The Book of James

MIKE HILSON

Published by Wesleyan Publishing House
Indianapolis, Indiana 46250
Printed in the United States of America
ISBN: 978-1-63257-326-1
ISBN (e-book): 978-1-63257-327-8

This book was previously self-published as *Coffee with the Pastor: the book of James.*

Names: Hilson, Mike, author.
Title: The book of James / Mike Hilson.
Description: Indianapolis, Indiana : Wesleyan Publishing House, [2019] |
Series: Coffee with the pastor | "This book was previously self-published as Coffee with the pastor: the book of James." | Includes bibliographical references. |
Identifiers: LCCN 2019014010 (print) | LCCN 2019018106 (ebook) | ISBN 9781632573278 () | ISBN 9781632573261 | ISBN 9781632573278 (ebk.)
Subjects: LCSH: Bible. James--Commentaries.
Classification: LCC BS2785.53 (ebook) | LCC BS2785.53 .H55 2019 (print) | DDC 227/.91077--dc23
LC record available at https://lccn.loc.gov/2019014010

Contents

Acknowledgments

Thank you to my wife, Tina, who has been my partner in life and in ministry. I love you!

To our three boys, Robert, Stephen, and Joshua, thank you for taking this journey of ministry with us and having a great attitude about it along the way.

Thank you also to my family at New Life Wesleyan Church for giving me the freedom to grow as a leader and as a follower of Christ.

Most importantly, I want to thank and praise God!

About This Book

People sometimes ask why I would take the time to write a book. The answer is twofold. First, it's an opportunity to speak with my children, grandchildren, and great-grandchildren about this wonderful gospel that I have had the honor of working for all of my life. I want them to see the joy and power of living a life guided and protected by God's Word, God's Spirit, and God's commands. In doing so, I hope to establish many generations of my family in the wonderful grace of our Lord. So I write as a father.

I also write as a pastor. New Life Wesleyan Church has become a rather large body of believers meeting in multiple services and multiple locations across multiple states. While this is a huge reason to praise God and more of a blessing than any of us who work here could ever have hoped for, it creates its own set of challenges. It has become impossible for me to sit down individually with folks in the church like I once did and have deeper conversations about the power of God's Word and how it can be applied in their lives. And so, this is the reason for a series of books called *Coffee with the Pastor*.

While I am neither a theologian nor a scholar, as a pastor, it is my job to help people read and better understand the Word of God. His Word is powerful and life changing. If you read and understand it, you can see the God of heaven through the blood of Jesus and the power of the Holy Spirit—and that will change your life. Therefore, the goal of this series of books is not theological, but a practical application of life-changing, biblical truth. That is the purpose of my ministry and the ultimate goal of my life.

So, grab a cup of coffee, open up your Bible, and let us think about what God can do in your life.

Introduction

James, a servant of God and of the Lord Jesus Christ.

—James 1:1

The opening line tells us the name of the author of this epistle (letter). However, several men in the New Testament are named James. So which one wrote this letter? One commentator explains it this way. "There were two apostles with the name of James. One was the brother of John, son of Zebedee. The other was the son of Alphaeus (see Matt. 10:2–3). However, neither of them is thought to have been the author of this Epistle. The oldest half-brother of Jesus was also named James (see Matt. 13:55). . . . Most scholars believe that he wrote this general letter."[1] So James, the brother of Jesus, is generally thought to be the writer of this epistle.

One second-century writer described James in this way:

James, the brother of the Lord, who, as there were many of this name, was surnamed the Just by all, from the days of our lord until now, received the government of the Church with the apostles. This man was holy from his mother's womb. He drank neither wine nor strong drink, and abstained from animal food. A

> razor never came upon his head, he never anointed himself with oil, and never used a bath. He alone was allowed to enter the sanctuary. He never wore woolen, but linen garments. He was in the habit of entering the temple alone, and was often found upon his bended knees, and asking for the forgiveness of the people; so that his knees became as hard as camels', in consequence of his habitual supplication and kneeling before God.[2]

And so, we have an epistle written by someone who by his family, upbringing, training, and personal example is worthy of our attention. In fact, among the early church leaders that we know much more about, this lesser-known character carried a huge reputation. Clement of Alexandria, the ancient historian, recorded this concerning St. James' appointment to the charge of the church of Jerusalem: "Peter and James and John, after the ascension of our Saviour, did not contend for the honour, but chose James the Just as Bishop of Jerusalem."[3]

In the last part of verse 1, James wrote to Jewish people ("the twelve tribes") who no longer lived in Israel or Jerusalem ("scattered among the nations"). This knowledge can help us understand the cultural assumptions behind James' words. He spoke into Jewish culture and was most comfortable with Jewish culture. In Acts 15:12–21, James helped bring resolution to an early conflict about the requirements for non-Jewish people who entered the Christian faith. While James had a deep understanding and appreciation for the traditional Jewish customs and laws, he also understood the unique needs of non-Jewish believers.

PART 1

JAMES 1

1

Consider it pure joy, my brothers and sisters,
whenever you face trials of many kinds.
—James 1:2

On the surface, this requirement seems very odd. Why would we consider it joy to face trials? The word *joy* really does mean what it seems to mean. The original Greek word *chara* refers to the actual emotion of joy or gladness or an occasion that brings joy or gladness.[1] Here, the apostle is requiring us to have the actual emotion of joy or gladness as a result of facing trials. This request seems unreasonable until we read in verse 3 that "the testing of your faith produces perseverance."

Every trial has a purpose, just like every heartache has a benefit and scar a lesson. When we face "trials of many kinds," we encounter life lessons. Each trial teaches us something or strengthens us in some way. Whatever we may think of the statement, it is still true: "What doesn't kill you, makes you stronger." This type of understanding gives meaning to our trials and purpose to our suffering. We are not just in anguish; we are learning. Learning to be stronger, smarter, calmer, and wiser. None of this knowledge eases the pain and heartache of trials; however, that pain and heartache is somewhat easier to endure when we know there is purpose behind it.

Let perseverance finish its work so that you may be mature and complete, not lacking anything.

—James 1:4

Just as individual trials make us stronger, the repetitive occurrence of trials builds our perseverance and character. Over time, strength builds on top of strength until we become truly resilient, wise, powerful, strong, "mature and complete." With enough time (and it will take a lot of time) and through the grace of God, the presence of the Holy Spirit, and the maturity that comes from enduring trials, we can come to a place of "not lacking anything." This maturing process takes time, and tough lessons must be learned along the way. At times, we might be tempted to lose our perspective and quit. The apostle speaks to that as well, when he said anyone lacking wisdom should ask our God, who does not find fault and gives generously (v. 5).

When the going is tough and the pain and difficulty are mounting, we can easily lose our perspective on the work God is doing in us. We can focus on the pain and forget about the progress. In these moments, we must cry out to God and ask him for wisdom. We must ask for the wisdom to understand that he is working in our lives and to remember that every trial has a beginning and an ending. Trials come, and trials go.

God sustains us through each one. When we ask God to give us wisdom to retain our perspective, he "gives generously to all without finding fault."

It is difficult to explain how comforting those words are to me. That God would give me the wisdom that I lack and do it without finding fault in me is a marvelous thought. I can be so weak and lose perspective so easily. But without yelling at me, calling me stupid, looking down on me, or judging me in any way, God gives generously. What an amazing grace! What an amazing God!

But when you ask, you must believe and not doubt, because the one who doubts is like a wave of the sea, blown and tossed by the wind. That person should not expect to receive anything from the Lord. Such a person is double-minded and unstable in all they do.

—James 1:6–8

Faith ultimately requires faith. That might seem redundant, but sometimes we all need a reminder of that simple truth. We want a steady, regular, predictable relationship with the Creator God of the universe. We want him to do exactly what we expect, when we expect it, and how we expect it to be done. We want God to work like a business contract or a vending machine—if I do these things, I will get these results. But God doesn't work that way.

This chapter presents a clear theme: trials . . . perseverance . . . maturity . . . completeness . . . wisdom . . . and for all of that . . . faith!

This is not a prescription for getting a new car, a new house, or a big raise. It is a prescription for *becoming*, not getting. God wants us to become more, better, wiser, stronger, deeper, and more like him! That process is not predictable or steady. Life has ups and downs. There are good days and bad days, trials and blessings. We need to ask for wisdom—when it is all going right and when it is all going wrong. When we ask for wisdom, we must ask with belief. Our faith in God is what ultimately provides the wisdom we need and gives us the courage and stability to carry on when a given moment doesn't make sense.

When we falter in our faith, we become unstable. We're blown about like the waves of the sea on a stormy day, furious and flustered, while God is in the deep parts of our lives, untouched by the fury that seems to be tearing us apart. Our faith reminds us that the wind and storm will eventually stop. Then the surface will be just as calm as the depths. What is really deep inside will come through on top.

Maturity, peace, strength, and faith will prevail. Confusion, doubt, indecisiveness, disillusionment, and depression will fade away with the passing wind and leave us further convinced that our faith is placed, not vainly in a God that does not respond, but wisely in *the* God who cares and delivers.

Believers in humble circumstances ought to take pride in their high position.
—James 1:9

Perspective is one of the most important things we can achieve in life. On day one, we spoke of our perspective of God and his delivering power. In today's verses, we deal with our perspective of ourselves in light of that same delivering power. God's power, presence, and favor entirely change our perspectives on life.

Growing up, I lived in a small town named Mt. Ulla. People just a few miles away did not even know the town existed. I developed a perspective that I often still refer to today: "Ain't nobody. Ain't from nowhere. Ain't never done nothing." That perspective at first was a depressing thought. It was born out of feeling a bit trapped in my small town, small bank account, and small future world. At least, that is how I perceived it.

I thought I would spend the rest of my life just trying to scratch out some type of living until I could finally retire and scratch out some kind of end to this small life, in this small world. Now, don't get me wrong; what I was facing was only partially depressing. I always have been aware that any honest work is good work and any God-given life is a good life. I knew that there would be immeasurable value in my life and that

God would use me and those around me in really cool ways. Yet, I still saw my world through the lens of: "Ain't nobody. Ain't from nowhere. Ain't never done nothing."

Then God got ahold of my perspective.

I began to realize that because of how I saw myself, I was perfectly positioned to be the one God wanted to use. When I was defined by, "Ain't nobody. Ain't from nowhere. Ain't never done nothing," God got all the glory for anything I accomplished. I didn't need to be rich or powerful to be of value. I *needed* God. I had no hope or opportunity without him.

I remember being in prayer one day, scheming with God on how I would create more opportunity in my life. I distinctly remember the voice of God in my spirit saying to me, "Michael, you take care of the ministry, and I will take care of the opportunity." At that, I just went back to my office, stopped scheming, and started working.

Hear me: Your humble circumstances should not be seen as a *limitation*; they should be seen as an *opportunity*. Those circumstances have you perfectly positioned to become an incredible praise report to the glory of God. You *need* him, and that is awesome!

But the rich should take pride in their humiliation—since they will pass away like a wild flower. For the sun rises with scorching heat and withers the plant; its blossom falls and its

beauty is destroyed. In the same way, the rich will fade away even while they go about their business.

—James 1:10–11

Now, that does not mean that those who are well-positioned, well-funded, well-educated, and well-provided with opportunity should somehow believe that they do not need God. On the contrary, they should understand the passing nature of their wealth and success.

Consider this: Without God, we are just creatures passing through this world. The forces around us will toss us, batter us, comfort us, entertain us, whatever with us. We have no control over any of it. Just when we think we have it all under control, the forces surrounding us somehow remind us that we really are not in control—sickness, economic downturn, natural disaster, or whatever else will remind us we are temporary on this planet. That can be frightening, depressing, limiting, confusing, . . . and then it starts to sound a lot like, "Ain't nobody. Ain't from nowhere. Ain't never done nothing."

In fact, no matter who you are, where you are from, or what you have accomplished, you *need* God. Sometimes, those who seem to have it all, have a more difficult time realizing their need for him. But life has a way of reminding us.

So, let me make this really simple: If you have no name, history, accomplishments, resources, or future, then that makes you perfectly positioned to be used by God. Praise God for that!

If you have an important last name, an impressive family line, an impressive resume, strong resources, and endless possibility sitting right in front of you, then praise God because you still "Ain't nobody. Ain't from nowhere. Ain't never done nothing." And that makes you perfectly positioned to be used by God!

3

Blessed is the one who perseveres under trial because, having stood the test, that person will receive the crown of life that the Lord has promised to those who love him.

—James 1:12

God truly honors those who stand strong under trial and temptation. The phrase *crown of life* is found in only one other place in Scripture. In the book of Revelation, John the Revelator, was taken up into heaven and saw the glorified Jesus standing among lampstands and stars, representing the churches of that day. Each church was either condemned or commended for its actions. The church of Smyrna was commended: "I know your afflictions and your poverty—yet you are rich!" (Rev. 2:9). They had remained true, even in great difficulty. Faithfulness under affliction made these people "rich" in the eyes of God, and that blessing was to extend beyond this life. "Do not be afraid of what you are about to suffer. I tell you, the devil will put some of you in prison to test you, and you will suffer persecution for ten days. Be faithful, even to the point of death, and I will give you life as your victor's crown" (Rev. 2:10). God would honor their faithfulness for all eternity and mark them as having suffered and stood the test!

Given this, we can understand why the apostle called those who persevere under trial "blessed." Our culture does not comprehend this. Our modern perspective says that if perseverance is required and trials and temptations are present, then obviously we are doing something wrong. From that perspective, blessing, rest, comfort, peace, happiness, and fun should be the mark of a life lived well.

But that isn't how God thinks. God looks at us and desires to see us stand firm in him no matter what. He wants us to find a joy and peace in him that can endure even in dark and difficult days. Yes, there will be good, easy days. However, those who can endure the tough, dark days, and do so while retaining the joy and peace of Christ in their hearts, are truly blessed!

In verse 13, we are reminded that trials and temptations are inevitable. In our attempt to explain why, we may say things like, "Well, God must have sent that to test me." Be careful with phrases like this. God does not tempt anyone! God's goal is not to trap you and see whether he can knock you off of your faith path. God isn't like that, and thank God he isn't! God's goal for our lives is for us to be true followers of him and live in a deep, real relationship with him. Temptations do not come from God; they are enticed by a really familiar source—our own evil desire (v. 14).

Yep, that's right! Those temptations are ours. This can be a real bummer. You can't even blame the devil! Those temptations are yours. They are born in you. You feed them, nurture them, give in to them, and strengthen them. They are truly yours.

Many in our culture want someone or something to blame for their own failures. They blame their DNA, parents, family, church, school, culture, government. They will blame anything or anyone else, as long as they do not have to blame themselves. They would rather be victims than failures. The truth is that we do not have to be either. In Christ, we can be blessed and given a crown of life, if we endure rather than give in to our temptations.

Then, after desire has conceived, it gives birth to sin; and sin, when it is full-grown, gives birth to death.

—James 1:15

The imagery here is so vivid. Our own desires *drag* us away and *entice* us to do wrong, and when we repeatedly give in to them, that temptation is *conceived* and born into a real life sin. That sin then grows like a cancer in our spiritual lives until it finally brings death.

Death is always the result of sin.

While the result of sin may not be physical death, a death of some sort will follow the repetitive surrender to sin. Sin is sneaky. At first, it seems to bring peace, happiness, and fun. For a while, we enjoy the sin. Then we begin to yearn for the sin. That yearning leads us to *need* the sin, and ultimately, the sin owns us. This pattern holds true in all kinds of sinfulness, from lying to cheating, from drinking to sex; the insidious process of death that is released when we give in to sin is real and is truly deadly.

But there is good news!

4

Don't be deceived, my dear brothers and sisters.

—James 1:16

Deception is real and prevalent in the world in which we live. Most of our culture is fully deceived by sin. We define *sin* as fun. When we use words like *party* or *break* or *fun*, they most often suggest some type of sinful activity. This fundamental shift in our cultural thinking is incredibly dangerous. It has infiltrated our church culture as well. What was once unthinkable within church and congregational culture is now often expected.

I remember a day, and I am not that old, when it was virtually unthinkable that a couple would come to the church to get married when they were already living together. This would have been scandalous. Today, most of the weddings we perform in the church involve couples who are already living together. In fact, when we point out that a biblical understanding of sex demands that sex remain only within the bond of marriage, most couples are shocked. They never knew that, or at least never thought that the Bible really meant that. And yet, sin is still sinful. The Bible has not changed but culture has . . . and now the church has changed too. This type of shift is almost never a good thing. We have allowed ourselves to become utterly deceived by the teaching of this world to the point that the Bible seems weird, out of touch, odd, or completely confusing. The apostle implores us to not be deceived. Sin is sin, and sin is deadly. Stay away from it!

But James offers hope.

Every good and perfect gift is from above, coming down from the Father of the heavenly lights, who does not change like shifting shadows.

—James 1:17

God is always good! Following God's prescription for our lives is always healing and helpful. God gives good and perfect gifts to those who will follow him. He gives health, peace, joy, prosperity, and strength to those who will chase his truth instead of the world's feelings and opinions. God's truth is not like culture's opinions. Culture changes its mind almost constantly. What is cool today is passé tomorrow. What is right today is wrong tomorrow. What is good today is bad tomorrow.

But God is not like that! He "does not change like shifting shadows." God's ways are right and true. They always have been and always will be. Culture with all of its reasoned arguments cannot remove the truth from Truth or the righteousness from

Rightness. "Don't be deceived"; instead, receive "good and perfect" gifts. The difference is in whom you choose to follow.

Culture follows sin, which leads to death.

Christians follow God, who leads to life!

The *birth* referred to in verse 18 does not refer to when our mothers birthed us. No, this birth is spiritual; some would call it a *second birth*. Jesus spoke to Nicodemus about this when he said, "No one can see the kingdom of God unless they are born again" (John 3:3). Nicodemus asked the obvious question, "How can someone be born when they are old?" to which Jesus explained, "No one can enter the kingdom of God unless they are born of water and the Spirit. Flesh gives birth to flesh, but the Spirit gives birth to spirit" (John 3:4–6).

This is the process that we refer to as "getting saved." At our church, we explain this as the ABCs.

Admit: I have sinned and need forgiveness.

"For all have sinned and fall short of the glory of God" (Rom. 3:23).

Believe: Jesus can and will forgive my sins.

"If you declare with your mouth 'Jesus is Lord' and believe in your heart that God raised him from the dead, you will be saved" (Rom. 10:9).

Commit: Change my ways to his ways.

"Repent, then, and turn to God, so that your sins may be wiped out, that times of refreshing may come from the Lord" (Acts 3:19).

Receive Christ as your Savior and don't be deceived by sin anymore!

In verse 18, God shows us to the rest of the world as an example of what he can do in and through everyone else. The *firstfruits* was an offering given by Israel's farmers. At harvest, the first handful of grains, still on the stalk, were taken to the priest. The priest would raise the grain toward heaven and wave it, signifying that glory was given to God for this produce. The very first of that harvest had been given to God for his glory. In the same way, God wants to take each and every one of us, raise us up in front of everyone, and declare all he has accomplished in our lives. He wants to show the healing and cleansing he has brought about in our lives. He wants to make us the firstfruits of all that he intends to accomplish in the field that produced us and contains all of our friends, family, and loved ones.

He wants to start with us, and from there, reach our world!

5

My dear brothers and sisters, take note of this: Everyone should be quick to listen, slow to speak and slow to become angry.

—James 1:19

Up to this point in his letter, James has encouraged Christians to change the way we *think* about the world and our lives. Joy in trials, blessing in perseverance, death from sin, freedom from deception caused by cultural understandings of sin, good and perfect gifts from above—all of these have to do with the way we think. At this point, James shifts to talking about how these truths should affect what we *do* and the way we *live*. This epistle is brutally honest and practical.

And the practical teaching begins now in verse 19.

"Everyone should be quick to listen, slow to speak and slow to become angry." Now that is some good advice! All too often, we do just the opposite. We are quick to speak, slow to listen, and quick to become angry. In fact, those three things naturally run in that order. When we speak too quickly, we tend to trap ourselves in a statement or position that isn't right. Rather than listening to truth, we immediately begin defending our original statement or opinion. This leads to anger, because we cannot understand why the other party doesn't comprehend our position. All the while, we have been slow to listen to the actual conversation that is going on. This describes far too many marriages, families, work places, and churches!

In his commentary on the epistle of James, J. Vernon McGee gives the following insight:

> The story is told about Socrates and a young man who was brought to him to enter his school. . . . The young man came in and was introduced to Socrates. Before he could say a word, the young man started talking. . . . When the young man finished, Socrates said, "I'll take you as a student, but I'm going to charge you twice as much." The young man asked, "Why are you going to charge me double?" Socrates' reply was this: "First I am going to have to teach you how to hold your tongue and then how to use it."[1]

It would do us all good to "be quick to listen, slow to speak, and slow to become angry."

Keep in mind that being quick to listen and slow to speak will actually help you avoid anger (v. 20). "Listen more and talk less" is a great formula for avoiding unnecessary outbursts of anger. This is important, because those outbursts of anger do not produce what God wants to see in our lives. God is moving us toward peace, patience, endurance, perseverance, forgiveness, and love. None of these are enhanced by angry outbursts. The righteousness that God desires from us is best produced when we are listening more, talking less, and rarely angry.

Therefore, get rid of all moral filth and the evil that is so prevalent and humbly accept the word planted in you, which can save you.

—James 1:21

Each of us allows something to be planted in us on a daily basis. Whatever is planted in us is exactly what will grow out of us. For example, when we allow inappropriate talk or images to enter our ears and eyes on a daily basis, those seeds are planted inside our hearts and minds. Over time, they take root. If they are consistently watered with a continual flow of more inappropriate talk and images, they begin to flourish and will ultimately take over our personal and spiritual lives.

This seed imagery answers a question raised by this verse. The apostle calls us to "get rid of all moral filth and evil." The way we do this is managing the input into our hearts and minds.

It is not unlike how I manage my lawn. Every season when it is appropriate, I plant new grass seed. Then, at the right time, I will go around and kill as many weeds as I can. Over time, I end up with a yard that has far more grass and far less weeds. Our spiritual lives work the same way. Some folks will tell you to spend all your time digging out all the sinful weeds in your life, but that just leaves you focused on the negative and that can become discouraging. Others say, don't worry about the sinful weeds and just plant new spiritual seeds. However, that leaves the damaging weeds of sin to multiply uninhibited and can ultimately cause hypocrisy and failure. The answer is to work on both.

There are times when it is appropriate to dig out, however painful it may be to do so, the weeds of sin that have so long taken root in our lives. There are other times when it is appropriate to generously spread the new seeds of righteousness throughout the lawn of our spiritual lives. Weed and seed! Do both! And do them often!

6

Do not merely listen to the word, and so deceive yourselves. Do what it says.
—James 1:22

The greatest threat to Christianity, in my opinion, is not atheism, but lukewarm Christians. Christians who claim to know Christ, attend church regularly, and even tithe and serve in the church, but don't allow the truth of the Word and the power of the Spirit to make any actual changes in their lives, are an internal threat to the spread of the gospel. Jesus must have felt much the same way. As Jesus spoke to the apostle John in the book of Revelation, he revealed how he felt about the situation. In speaking to the church in Laodicea, he said this: "I know your deeds, that you are neither cold nor hot. I wish you were either one or the other! So, because you are lukewarm—neither hot nor cold—I am about to spit you out of my mouth" (Rev. 3:15–16). Unchanged, unmoved Christians literally make Jesus sick.

We cannot just listen to the Word of God and politely nod in agreement. We need to do something about it. Remember, those who listen to God's Word but don't apply it, may be proclaiming Christianity, but practicing atheism.

Anyone who listens to the word but does not do what it says is like someone who looks at his face in a mirror and, after looking at himself, goes away and immediately forgets what he looks like.

—James 1:23–24

This *practical atheism* has a consequence in the church. Spanning decades, the church has consistently trended toward being more and more like the culture around it. This should not be surprising to us. There is always a tendency to morph our belief system into the culture we find comfortable. There is always a temptation to rationalize our way out of commands and laws that we don't like. Therefore, over time, the church looks increasingly like the culture and all of the necessary, distinct parts of Christianity fade away. In an attempt to take the *offense* out of the gospel, we take the *power* out of the gospel.

When this occurs, Christians forget what they are supposed to look like. When we stop trying to look and act like the Christ of Scripture, we begin trying to look and act like whatever celebrity we happen to be following at the moment. This is tricky stuff. Soon enough, that celebrity fades or is disgraced, and we are forced to choose a new one. Then that one changes for some reason as well and we have to find another. Before long, we end up chasing so many "role models" that we are no longer sure what we are supposed to look like, and we have absolutely no idea who we really are.

With Christ, it isn't like that. You can *never* be exactly like Christ. He is perfect; you are not. He is God; you are not. He is risen; you are not. He is Judge; you are not.

When we follow Christ, he brings out of us the very best person that God intended for us from the beginning. He makes you a better you. He makes you a sanctified you. Then, when you look in the mirror, you will not see a cheap imitation of a poor "role model"; you will look in the mirror of Scripture and see the sanctified, cleansed, chosen, and healed you that God has always seen.

But whoever looks intently into the perfect law that gives freedom, and continues in it—not forgetting what they have heard, but doing it—they will be blessed in what they do.

—James 1:25

All of this leads to blessing. Quite frankly, this blessing is a natural outcome of actually following and doing what God says we should follow and do. He knows what is best for us, and he is trying to lead us into what is best for us. We simply have to surrender to his ways.

As I preach, I often attempt to emphasize this point: Far too many Christians are looking for some lightning bolt of a miracle in their lives. They want some kind of extraterrestrial experience with God that just sets them free from everything that could ever slow them down. However, God, most often, doesn't work like that.

God wants us to look "intently into the perfect law that gives freedom" so that we will naturally know the right thing to do. The longer we do that, the more we will build right things into our lives. Blessing is best summed up as the cumulative effect of constantly building right things into our lives. The more we build right things, the more we are blessed. The more we build wrong things (sin), the more we are cursed. It just makes sense! For that reason, we must not merely listen to the word, and so deceive ourselves. We must do what it says.

7

Those who consider themselves religious and yet do not keep a tight rein on their tongues deceive themselves, and their religion is worthless.

—James 1:26

The word *religious* is an interesting word and sets the tone for today's thoughts. The Greek word used by the apostle is really quite rare and is not used anywhere else in Scripture. The word is *threskos*. One commentator described the word this way: "It is difficult to find an English word which exactly answers to the Greek. The noun . . . refers properly to the external rites of religion, and so gets to signify an over-scrupulous devotion to external forms . . . ; almost ritualism."[1] The *Strong's Greek Dictionary* defines this word as "Ceremonious in worship (as demonstrative); i.e. pious: — religious."[2]

And so, unpacking this meaning of the word in the context of the apostle's writing, we arrive at an interesting realization. He was speaking about people who *think* they are religious, because of their ceremonial following of certain rites or traditions, but who are really quite *irreligious*, because they do not really know the Christ of Scripture. Now, to be quite honest, our churches are filled with these types of people. Many believe that just because they attend services or give a little money or do a little "Christian" work once in a while, they are saved.

I have had people declare to me that God will need to let them into heaven because of their good works.

Friends, hear me carefully; you *cannot* earn your way into heaven.

Christianity is not a set of religious practices that must be followed, with exact rites and rituals. Christianity, rightly understood, is a relationship with the Creator God of heaven that has been opened up by the cleansing blood of Jesus and the constant presence of the Holy Spirit. Whatever practices and rituals proceed from that relationship can truly be called Christianity. Practices and rituals that proceed from fear or empty religion cannot rightly be called Christianity. We must have more than just ritual. We must have a relationship.

One of the ways you can know that your Christianity is in trouble and likely not deep enough to make a difference in your life or in the world around you, is the way in which you control your tongue. If your mouth is out of control, your "religion" is worthless. There really are two reasons this may be true. From an internal/spiritual perspective, if your relationship with God and your surrender to the Holy Spirit is not complete enough to control your mouth, then it is lacking something. That kind of religion is worthless to you as an individual. There is no internal change, strength, or spiritual growth. If there were such growth, then you would have better control of your mouth. From an external/public perspective, if your mouth undoes everything your faith and actions are trying to convey, your faith and actions are worthless. In fact, they are worse than worthless. They are causing damage to the overall perception that those around you have of the kingdom of God. Your worthless faith is giving your priceless Savior a bad name.

> *Religion that God our Father accepts as pure and faultless is this: to look after orphans and widows in their distress and to keep oneself from being polluted by the world.*
>
> —James 1:27

The apostle clearly and simply spells out for us what a real relationship with the God of heaven will produce in our lives. True religion—a true relationship with God—changes our perspective of the world around us. Rather than seeing it as our own personal playground where we constantly strive to get all we can get, we begin to see the needs of others and the righteousness of Christ. It is true religion that causes us finally to see the important things in our lives. Again, one of my favorite commentaries had this to say about it: "Observe that our duty towards our fellow-men is placed first; then that towards ourselves."[3] In another favorite commentary of mine, Dr. McGee precisely expresses a problem that we should all be deeply concerned about: "I feel there is a grave danger in our having a religion of the sanctuary but not a religion of the street."[4]

In order to fight against such a worthless religion, we must find more than just empty rituals and self-serving services. Going to church will not change you. Giving away money will not change you. Ritualistic ways will not change you. A real experience and relationship with the Creator God of heaven through the blood of the sacrificial Savior, Jesus, and the presence and power of the Holy Spirit, will not only change you, it will change the world around you.

PART 2

JAMES 2

8

My brothers and sisters, believers in our glorious Lord Jesus Christ must not show favoritism. Suppose a man comes into your meeting wearing a gold ring and fine clothes, and a poor man in filthy old clothes also comes in. If you show special attention to the man wearing fine clothes and say, "Here's a good seat for you," but say to the poor man, "You stand there" or "Sit on the floor by my feet," have you not discriminated among yourselves and become judges with evil thoughts?

—James 2:1–4

The message in these verses is very straightforward and simple, yet we seem to get this one wrong a lot. First of all, let's understand the command here. The apostle is giving a very simple instruction: We "must not show favoritism." He then gives us an example of what he is talking about. In his example, he cites a common form of favoritism. People like to be associated with or friends with rich, successful people. Church people are no exception to this rule. Therefore, the apostle gives a wonderful example to teach his point.

Sometimes as Christians, we miss the point of what he is saying here altogether. I have watched as celebrity pastors fawn over rich, famous, and powerful people who show up at church or somehow claim a life-changing experience with Christ. Now, sometimes that experience is real and their lives are actually changed. And sometimes, well, not so much. In the end, what is unseemly and unchristian is fawning over the wealthy, famous, and powerful while overlooking the poor, downcast, and average. No cameras ever follow poor widows and orphans around. No paparazzi are chasing homeless folks. No glossy magazine is spending millions to capture images of the average Joes and Janes who are scratching out an existence in this world. No, the cameras are looking for the rich, the powerful, and the famous. Unfortunately, sometimes, so is the church.

Church leaders want to build buildings, pay bills, gain entry into special circles of people, be seen as successful or powerful themselves, or be celebrities themselves. Whatever the reason, it is too often true that church leaders chase after the rich and do so to the detriment of the poor, and the gospel.

Sometimes the same principle is played out on a much smaller and less-obvious scale. We don't want kids from challenged neighborhoods in our youth group because they might lead our kids astray. We don't want people who can't dress right, talk right, and act right in our congregations, because they might run away the good folk who pay for stuff. We sometimes attempt to choose our culture and then reject those who don't fit in the culture we have chosen. That is showing favoritism. However, this is not the only way we miss the apostle's point.

I have also watched as Christian leaders rejected and ignored people of wealth simply because they have wealth.

This, too, is showing favoritism. I have watched Christian leaders refuse to minister in certain neighborhoods because "those people are too wealthy to need God." I have watched attitudes play out in evangelistic strategies that focus so completely on the poor that the middle class and wealthy are entirely ignored. I have had debates with folks who simply insist on defining *urban* as poor. While some urban areas are poor, many are not. It is possible to overreact to the apostle's command here and get it completely wrong.

Look, it is really very simple: Jesus died for *all* people, so don't just reach out to rich people! If you do, you are being a jerk (selective and not true to the Word)!

Jesus died for *all* people, so don't just reach out to poor people! If you do, you are *still* being a jerk (selective and not true to the Word)!

Jesus died for *all* people so reach them—*all* of them. If you do, you are being a servant of the Most High!

9

Listen, my dear brothers and sisters: Has not God chosen those who are poor in the eyes of the world to be rich in faith and to inherit the kingdom he promised those who love him? But you have dishonored the poor. Is it not the rich who are exploiting you? Are they not the ones who are dragging you into court? Are they not the ones who are blaspheming the noble name of him to whom you belong?

—James 2:5–7

It is a true statement that the poor are mistreated in virtually every aspect of society, including the church. Yet God has "chosen those who are poor in the eyes of the world to be rich in faith and to inherit the kingdom" (v. 5). Simply put, your place in society has no bearing at all on your place in the kingdom of God. The apostle Paul says a similar thing in 1 Corinthians 1:27–29: "But God chose the foolish things of the world to shame the wise; God chose the weak things of the world to shame the strong. God chose the lowly things of this world and the despised things—and the things that are not—to nullify the things that are, so that no one may boast before him." God uses the weakest, poorest, most unknown, and ill-placed people to accomplish great things in his kingdom. He does this so that the world will clearly see that it is *his* greatness, grace, power, and goodness that brings all these things about.

It is true that the rich and powerful strive to hold down the poor and powerless. This is true, and it always has been true, in every culture and every country on the face of the planet. Communism is perfectly designed to keep common people in their place. Socialism is perfectly designed to keep poor people in their place. Capitalism is perfectly designed to allow the rich to effectively take from anyone and everyone else. Every culture does this. The ones in power take from the ones out of power. Every culture, that is, except true Christian culture.

In today's world, many would argue that the altruistic government must control rich corporations in order to protect the poor citizens. Now, it is true that corporations exist to take resources from anywhere else and bring them into the rich corporation. That is the very nature of capitalism. However, one thing must be perfectly understood. The government is anything but altruistic. Government and corporations are, in the end, the same things. They are both massive organizational systems that have completely self-centered motives. Like most organizations, they exist for the purpose of ensuring the existence of the organization. The larger the organization gets, the more focused it will become on ensuring its own long-term existence.

The corporation will ensure its long-term existence by securing an ever-increasing amount of financial input through business practice. This may come by selling more of a given product, selling a given product at a higher price, selling an increasing number of products, or simply increasing market dominance in a given product area. In order for the corporation to ensure its existence, it must make money—from you.

The government is only slightly different. In order to ensure the long-term existence of any given governmental agency, policy, or division, there must be an ever-lengthening list of things that agency, policy, or division defends or manages. Therefore, just as corporations will increase product in order to ensure their long-term existence, government will increase laws and regulations to ensure their continued long-term existence. In order to fund the enforcement of the ever-increasing number of laws and regulations, government will increase the tax load on its citizens to pay its employees to enforce its laws and regulations in order to ensure its continued existence. And those taxes are taken—from you.

So, in the end, both corporations and governments are taking from you. Both corporations and government have "dishonored the poor" consistently. Both corporations and government are "exploiting you." Both corporations and government are "the ones who are dragging you into court." Both corporations and government are consistently "blaspheming the noble name of him to whom you belong."

But the church should be different!

Whether we work in the corporate world or the government world, we should use our influence as Christians to be the arbiters of what is right and true and fair and good. We should be the hands and feet of Jesus in this world. People, systems, and organizations that are designed to take may dominate this world, but if we as the church are to follow the teachings of Christ, of Scripture, and of the apostle James here, we must be the ones who give, not take. We must be the ones who serve, not demand. We must be the ones who bring freedom, not bondage. They may serve a model that calls them to preserve their existence. We serve a Christ who calls us to give our lives.

We should be different!

10

If you really keep the royal law found in Scripture, "Love your neighbor as yourself," you are doing right.

—James 2:8

The teaching of Scripture should be fully evident to us on this point. Jesus declares it: "My command is this: Love each other as I have loved you" (John 15:12). The apostle Paul declares it: "And now these three remain: faith, hope and love. But the greatest of these is love" (1 Cor. 13:13). The apostle John declares it further in his letter to the church: "Dear friends, let us love one another, for love comes from God. Everyone who loves has been born of God and knows God" (1 John 4:7). The apostle Peter declares it in his letter to the church: "Above all, love each other deeply, because love covers over a multitude of sins" (1 Pet. 4:8). The writer of Hebrews declares it: "Keep on loving one another as brothers and sisters" (Heb. 13:1). The entirety of the New Testament seems to always lead us back to this one sentiment—to love each other just as Christ loved us.

It can be confusing to look at the church today in light of this. Far too often, we reject one another over simple differences of opinion, doctrine, or preference. We call each other names, and let each other down. We argue in the public courts over money, land, ownership, and reputation. All the while, the world looks at us and wonders why we hate each other so much. Nowhere in Scripture are we commanded to take up picket signs and say nasty things about other Christians or other humans for that matter. Nowhere are we commanded to reject a human being out of anger, and yet we do all these things.

Now some would say that they are protecting the purity of the church or the integrity of their little group by acting this way. They would argue that their righteousness in following the commands of Christ matters so much that this love one another thing just doesn't measure up in importance. However, to love one another is *clearly* a command of Jesus: "My command is this: Love each other as I have loved you" (John 15:12). Therefore, to break this command has the same consequence as breaking any other command, and the apostle James makes just that point!

But if you show favoritism, you sin and are convicted by the law as lawbreakers. For whoever keeps the whole law and yet stumbles at just one point is guilty of breaking all of it. For he who said, "You shall not commit adultery," also said, "You shall not murder." If you do not commit adultery but do commit murder, you have become a lawbreaker.

—James 2:9–11

Now, let's be clear: the apostle is not suggesting that by breaking a single command you would be guilty of breaking every command. What he is saying is that breaking any of the commands and laws of God makes you a lawbreaker by definition. If we are to truly believe that Jesus is God and that his Word constitutes law for us, then "love one another" is a command that we are obliged to follow just as much as "you shall not commit adultery" or "you shall not murder."

The church needs to grasp the reality of this truth. If we could ever truly understand that the call of God is to live in the tension between loving people and calling people to righteousness, we would be able to change the world around us. What if the world could hear our call to right biblical living from a voice of love and compassion? What if they knew we loved them even as we spoke difficult truth to them? What if even when we opposed them, they knew that our opposition was coming from a heart of love? How much more effective would that be?

I believe that is exactly what God is calling us to do. Love each other so that the world around us will know us by our love for one another. Then we can show them that this kind of perfect love comes from God. The result? Well, the apostle John summed that up quite well:

God is love. Whoever lives in love lives in God, and God in them. This is how love is made complete among us so that we will have confidence on the day of judgment: In this world we are like Jesus. There is no fear in love. But perfect love drives out fear, because fear has to do with punishment. The one who fears is not made in perfect love. We love because he first loved us.

—1 John 4:16–19

11

Speak and act as those who are going to be judged by the law that gives freedom, because judgment without mercy will be shown to anyone who has not been merciful. Mercy triumphs over judgment.

—James 2:12–13

In our daily lives, we must act toward everyone with mercy. This concept, like so many concepts and phrases found in the Epistles, comes directly from Jesus himself: "Do not judge, or you too will be judged. For in the same way you judge others, you will be judged, and with the measure you use, it will be measured to you" (Matt. 7:1–2).

The lesson here is very clear: We will be judged, and we will be shown mercy, based on how we ourselves have shown mercy or have been judgmental. While righteousness and rightly following the commands of God and the Word of God are an absolute requirement in Scripture, the Bible is also all about grace and mercy!

Life must be lived in the tension that exists between seemingly opposite yet real truths: grace is huge, and holiness is required. Both these statements are true, yet they seem to be opposites. They almost seem incapable of occupying the same theology, yet they quite fully define the theology of Christ. During his lifetime, Jesus implored his followers to live holy lives and follow God's ways. He called them to righteousness in every area of life and seemed to fully expect his closest followers to be successful in their attempt at holiness. He came "to seek and to save the lost" (Luke 19:10). He came to give his own life and shed his own blood to pay the debt of our sinfulness.

Jesus came to teach, model righteousness, and call people to a life of holiness. Jesus came to save the lost and give his life as ransom for the salvation of people who were not living lives of holiness. And so in the very life of Jesus, the tension is beautifully balanced out.

Grace is huge! It is the size of a cross on which the very Creator of the world chose to give his own life for the forgiveness of many whom had already long since rejected him.

Holiness is required! It is the requirement of our Savior who clearly said, "If you love me, keep my commands" (John 14:15).

Grace is huge! "But God demonstrates his own love for us in this: While we were still sinners, Christ died for us" (Rom. 5:8).

Holiness is required! "But just as he who called you is holy, so be holy in all you do; for it is written: 'Be holy, because I am holy'" (1 Pet. 1:15–16).

So, to sum up this simple lesson, don't be judgmental toward others or God will harshly judge you. In other words, mercy triumphs over judgment!

12

What good is it, my brothers and sisters,
if someone claims to have faith but has
no deeds? Can such faith save them?
—James 2:14

That is a sobering question. Can faith that has no physical outcome in deeds actually be a faith that saves? In essence, this is the question that the apostle is posing. The question raises all kinds of doctrinal dilemmas. So instead of wrestling with the doctrinal problems that are presented here, let me say two things that I think the apostle would clearly point out to us if he were here to discuss his writing.

1. Doing good deeds cannot win you salvation.

Scripture is clear on this point. "For it is by grace you have been saved, through faith—and this is not from yourselves, it is the gift of God—not by works, so that no one can boast" (Eph. 2:8–9). The apostle Paul, in these verses, gives the clearest defense against the thought of earned salvation. No one could possibly do enough good things to earn a spot in heaven. We just don't have the capacity for that kind of righteousness on our own. Salvation comes to us through the sacrificial blood of Jesus Christ our Savior and is made evident to our spirits through the indwelling Holy Spirit of God. So, "it is by grace you have been saved, through faith."

2. Salvation causes you to do good deeds.

Having said this, anyone who claims to have faith in Jesus Christ, but does nothing to serve him, is a liar. Now, I know that sounds harsh, but take a quick assessment of the question that the apostle James is asking here. Can a faith with no deeds actually bring salvation to a person's heart and life? The obvious assumption inherent in the question is *no*.

So, if you claim faith but do nothing about that faith, you should ask yourself if your faith is real or a lie. Quite frankly, *you* may be the one deceived by the lie. Satan is a cunning enemy. He will convince us that simply voicing faith in Christ is enough, when in fact, true faith will show itself in deeds. If Satan can convince us that we simply need to claim Christ and do nothing about our faith, he at the very least weakens us to the point that we are not helping anyone else find Christ, and at the very worst, he deceives us to the point that we have actually missed salvation.

Take assessment of your Christian faith and your Christian walk. Are you doing something about what you say you believe?

Suppose a brother or a sister is without clothes and daily food. If one of you says to them, "Go in peace; keep warm and well fed," but does nothing about their physical needs, what good is it?
—James 2:15–16

Think for a moment about the absolutely ridiculous nature of the scenario that the apostle just gave us. Imagine this in your modern-day world. Someone you know ends up homeless in the middle of winter. You speak with him at the mall. You know he has no food, no home to go to, and that when the mall closes its doors, he will spend the night out in the cold. Instead of doing anything about it, you walk away from him saying as you leave, "God bless you and keep you warm! Enjoy your dinner!" That is insulting, yet that is what faith without deeds looks like. Whether the need is spiritual, emotional, or physical, when the Holy Spirit confronts us with human need, we should be motivated by our faith to respond to that need. That does not mean that we buy everyone groceries, bring home every homeless person, or pay the late rent for every poor money manager we know. It does mean that we do something, because to do nothing draws our very faith into question.

The apostle spares no feelings as he assesses this situation and states that faith by itself is dead (v. 17). And faith that is dead is useless.

13

But someone will say,
"You have faith; I have deeds."
—James 2:18

I can't count the number of Christians I have met who live out this statement. Now, they would never actually say these words because they have read this verse, but they live out this reality. Some preacher or writer somewhere has convinced them that all they need is to just believe in Jesus, and then it doesn't matter what they do after. They are living out that promise. In fact, they love living out that promise.

Think about it. If all we must do is simply believe, and action is never required, well that's an awesome deal, and many people would take you up on that deal. Jesus is willing to die for me, shed blood for me, defend me before his Father, and build an eternal home for me—and he doesn't expect or demand anything from me?

That is ridiculous and is *not* biblical Christianity. By the way, it isn't a safe position to be in when facing eternity. "Can such faith save them?" (James 2:14). We honestly need fewer Christians of this type. They are doing damage to the name of Christ.

"Show me your faith without deeds, and I will show you my faith by my deeds" (James 2:18). We need more Christians like this! People who believe in Christ and act like Christ best advertise the reality of the true saving faith of Christ. When we serve the world around us in big and small ways, we speak the truth of the love of Christ to others. We show his love and his grace. That is the truth the world desperately needs to see from us. They have heard us declare our faith enough. They have heard us demand our way enough. They have heard us denounce their lifestyles enough. They desperately need to see us live out our lives like Christ in their presence.

Society changes when real people with real faith do real works that make a real difference in the real struggles of real people.

"Yes, Pastor, you make a good point. However, as long as I believe in Christ, I am saved and heaven-bound. That is good enough for me."

Really? So, if simply believing in Christ made you a saved, heaven-bound Christian, wouldn't that mean that all the demons in hell, and Satan himself, are saved, heaven-bound Christians (v. 19)? Think about that logic. Satan and all his demons fully and completely believe in and deeply fear God. They know Jesus and they "shudder" when they think of him. They believe, and they always have, but they are not saved. They are not heaven-bound. They are not Christians. The apostle James pulls no punches here when he clearly declares that when you use the "logic" that simple belief makes you a Christian, you are using hell-born, demon-approved logic that will leave you condemned and lost.

Believe . . . and then do something about it!

14

You foolish person, do you want evidence that faith without deeds is useless? Was not our father Abraham considered righteous for what he did when he offered his son Isaac on the altar? You see that his faith and his actions were working together, and his faith was made complete by what he did. And the scripture was fulfilled that says, "Abraham believed God, and it was credited to him as righteousness," and he was called God's friend. You see that a person is considered righteous by what they do and not by faith alone.

—James 2:20–24

The apostles would not have been very good televangelists. They were so incredibly blunt. Here, the apostle James calls this easy believe-ism what it actually is—foolishness. It is nonsense to believe that faith can be real if there is no result of deeds in our daily lives to evidence that faith. The apostle went back into the Old Testament, Jewish history, to prove his point.

The account that the apostle refers to is found in Genesis 22. It is honestly one of the most difficult stories in all Scripture. When you read this account, you must read it from an ancient perspective. In Abraham's day, people worshiped gods who demanded truly heinous acts. Child sacrifice was not uncommon. So when God asked Abraham to sacrifice his son, Isaac, God was literally asking Abraham to, by his actions, prove that he was as committed to the God of heaven as his neighbors were to their gods of wood and stone. Abraham passed the test.

Now, our God would *never* require us to actually sacrifice our children to him and his glory. Remember that! The question still stands as to whether we are as committed to our God of grace, peace, and love as others are to their gods of destruction, bloodshed, greed, pleasure, and death? They serve their gods with complete abandon, while it often seems we serve our God with complete ambivalence. They serve their gods to their own destruction, while it seems we struggle to serve our God even in the face of our own miraculous deliverance. Why is that? I think because we have bought into the lie of a faith that requires no deeds, and that faith is dead.

> *And in the same way was not also Rahab the prostitute justified by works when she received the messengers and sent them out by another way? For as the body apart from the spirit is dead, so also faith apart from works is dead.*
>
> —James 2:25–26 (ESV)

This story is found in Joshua 2. The prostitute Rahab protected two spies from the nation of Israel when they entered Jericho to spy secretly on the city. She did this at her own peril. The king of Jericho would surely have killed her and her entire household had he found out that she was hiding Jewish spies. Rahab understood something that I think we often forget. After she had hidden the spies on the roof of her house and sent the king's men out in the wrong direction, she told the two spies: "I know that the LORD has given you this land" (Josh. 2:9). She knew that the culture she lived in was doomed and that the God of heaven would ultimately prevail. She was willing to do whatever it took to ensure that she was on the side of the God of heaven when the battle was over. That was more than just knowing that the Israelites would win. That was more than just believing that the God of Israel would prevail. She was going to *do* whatever it took to be on God's side and find his mercy, grace, and promises shining down on her.

In the end, Rahab established the family line and ultimately had a place in the lineage of Jesus. Her actions brought generations of blessing to her offspring.

And so can ours!

JAMES 3

PART 3

15

Not many of you should become teachers,
my fellow believers, because you know that we
who teach will be judged more strictly.
—James 3:1

This word of warning should be taken to heart far more often than it is. Too many times, I run into people who want to "go into ministry." What they mean is that they want a new career. Quite frankly, many of them view vocational ministry in precisely that way—as just another career. Many people start with this kind of thinking: "If I get the degree and go to the right seminars and retreats, I can learn what I need to learn and have a career in ministry. I mean, I love church, so surely I would love working in the church!" The problem with this reasoning is that God, through the Holy Spirit, must call someone to ministry or it just isn't going to work out well.

One of the great challenges we face as a church is helping people differentiate between a love for doing ministry and a call for being in vocational ministry. These truly are different things. A simple love for ministry will not sustain someone through the really difficult times that always occur in ministry.

Further, and more damaging, when someone enters vocational ministry without a real call from the Holy Spirit, they lack the insight and fear that is necessary for rightly handling the Word of God and the people of God. You see, in the end that is what vocational ministry is all about. Rightly handling the Word of God and the people of God. To fail in either of these areas is an affront to the very heart of God! Let me unpack what I mean by insight and fear.

1. Insight from God

When the Holy Spirit calls someone to vocational ministry, he also inspires them and enlightens them in ways that are not fully explainable. You see, as vocational ministers we must teach the Word of God. That teaching requires insight and understanding that is not always available in books and seminars. Often, when I hear someone give a powerful sermon that just rocks a room, I will sit back and be amazed at what the Holy Spirit has revealed to that minister about the needs of all the individuals in the room. Other times, when I hear a powerfully entertaining sermon, I am impressed by the ability of the speaker to entertain. Both may have used Scripture. Both may have invoked the name of Jesus. Both may have had good motives. Only one of them communicated with the power of the Holy Spirit.

When a good communicator begins to lean on the strength of his own skills, that opens the door to heresy. If a person has powerful communication skills but a weak relationship with the Holy Spirit, then that person will begin teaching what they want to believe rather than what God said to believe. That can turn a skilled communicator into a cult leader.

2. Fear of God

This danger of falling into heresy must strike fear into the heart of anyone who takes on the task of teaching the Word of God. Honestly, any pastor worth his salt spends a great deal of time making sure he is saying right things in right ways. God is serious about his Word being taught properly. God is serious about his children being treated properly. When I run into a pastor or preacher who has no fear about what he does and says, I fear for that pastor! Listen to how Jesus describes the importance of this: "If anyone causes one of these little ones—those who believe in me—to stumble, it would be better for them to have a large millstone hung around their neck and to be drowned in the depths of the sea" (Matt. 18:6). Now if that doesn't strike fear into the heart of the pastor, then honestly the pastor should find a new career!

So, if you think perhaps you might want to be a pastor, preacher, or teacher, take a long hard look at this verse. Realize that you are taking on a responsibility that is so important to our Father in heaven that we are warned multiple times by multiple authors of the danger of doing it wrongly.

God will defend his Word!

God will defend his people!

Anyone who mishandles either has hell to pay!

We all stumble in many ways. Anyone who is never at fault in what they say is perfect, able to keep their whole body in check.

—James 3:2

Your tongue defines you. Here, the apostle takes a journey to an immensely practical place. How you speak truly defines who you are. In fact, the most difficult behavior to control is what comes out of our mouths. What people think of us is almost completely defined by what we say. Decades of hard work and kindness can be erased in seconds of harsh speech. Your tongue defines you.

We all know people who are completely kind. Maybe we have said something like, "I have never heard her say a harsh word about anybody!"

Think for just a moment. How do you feel about this person?

Likely you trust them, like being around them, enjoy talking to them, feel safe when you are with them, and know that you can confide in them when you are having personal trouble. In short, this is the type of person you really want to have around. If you have never heard them say a harsh word about anyone else, then it is highly likely that no one else has ever heard them say a harsh word about you. And therefore, you trust this person. Furthermore, you will defend this person. You would not want to say a harsh word about someone like this, nor would you allow someone else to say a harsh word about him or her.

Think about it. This is a recipe for being a trusted friend! Just control your mouth and you can be the trusted friend you have always wanted to have! The more you are that friend to others, the more likely you are to find that friend for yourself.

Now consider some other folks in your life. We all know people who just cannot seem to find nice things to say. They are foul-mouthed and critical. They seem to speak in angry, bitter tones, and they use words that are consistently cutting and negative.

Think for just a moment. How do you feel about this person? Likely, *trust* is not the word you would use. It would be wise not to share deep, dark secrets with such a person. You would do well not to let your guard down. Quite frankly, you likely don't want to spend large amounts of time around such a person. All of that is wise. Truth be told, if your friends are constantly talking bad about others when they are with you, then they are likely talking bad about you when you are not there. That would leave you feeling insecure, hurt, and broken.

Think about it. This is a recipe for not having friends.

Now, the truth is that your mouth defines you. It reveals you to be either someone others can trust or someone others should avoid. Whatever is true of your tongue today does not have to be true forever. God can forgive that filthy mouth of yours, and the Holy Spirit can change it!

You just have to let him.

When we put bits into the mouths of horses to make them obey us, we can turn the whole animal. Or take ships as an example. Although they are so large and are driven by strong winds, they are steered by a very small rudder wherever the pilot wants to go. Likewise, the tongue is a small part of the body, but it makes great boasts. Consider what a great forest is set on fire by a small spark. The tongue also is a fire, a world of evil among the parts of the body. It corrupts the whole body, sets the whole course of one's life on fire, and is itself set on fire by hell. All kinds of animals, birds, reptiles and sea creatures are being tamed and have been tamed by mankind, but no human being can tame the tongue. It is a restless evil, full of deadly poison.

—James 3:3–8

Your tongue controls you. Your tongue determines the trajectory of your life. Therefore, you need to get control of it!

The apostle here uses four different images to teach us the importance and danger of our uncontrolled mouths. In the first two, he teaches us a lesson that we would do well to learn. The bit in the horse's mouth will allow the rider to control the horse's direction. That bit is tiny in comparison to the size of the horse. In fact, the human riding the horse is actually no match for the animal he or she is now controlling. Still, a bit in a horse's mouth gives a weaker, smaller creature control of a larger, stronger animal.

Control the mouth, tame the beast.

A rudder on a ship is truly a small thing in comparison to the size and scope of the ship itself, and yet that tiny rudder is in control of where the ship goes. Tons and tons of metal, cargo, and hundreds or thousands of people are directed by a relatively tiny piece of metal under the control of a small wheel in the hand of one human.

Control the rudder, steer the ship.

That is exactly how your mouth works. It drives you. It directs you. It governs the trajectory of your very life. Your career can be enhanced or destroyed by the words you allow out of your mouth. Your marriage can be enhanced or destroyed by the words you allow out of your mouth. Your children can be enhanced or destroyed by the words you allow out of your mouth.

Something that powerful should be controlled!

However, it also must be understood that the tongue is a lot like a wildfire. It can be so easy to allow angry or hateful words to escape from our mouths, and it can be difficult or almost impossible to rid our minds and hearts completely of angry or hateful thoughts. Set ablaze by some small, insignificant occurrence, those thoughts and words can begin to grow and intensify until out of our mouths spew flamethrowers of anger that consume decades of beauty. All this destruction brings joy to the heart of hell.

Satan knows about your tongue, and he knows that he can use it to destroy your witness, career, family, kids, and even your faith. He will use it against you. All he needs to do is find you at a weak moment and set off some small spark of anger deep inside you. If he can nurture that little flame long enough, he will build up enough fuel inside of you to burn away all the good you have done.

You can't let him do that to you.

Controlling what comes out of our mouths begins by controlling what is allowed to fester in our hearts. Out of our mouths flow the very thoughts and beliefs of our hearts.

So, a clean mouth starts with a clean heart.

How are you doing?

18

With the tongue we praise our Lord and Father, and with it we curse human beings, who have been made in God's likeness. Out of the same mouth come praise and cursing. My brothers and sisters, this should not be. Can both fresh water and salt water flow from the same spring? My brothers and sisters, can a fig tree bear olives, or a grapevine bear figs? Neither can a salt spring produce fresh water.

—James 3:9–12

Your tongue blesses or buries.

In the Gospel of Luke, Jesus teaches us this very same principle when he says, "A good man brings good things out of the good stored up in his heart, and an evil man brings evil things out of the evil stored up in his heart. For the mouth speaks what the heart is full of" (6:45).

This is the secret to controlling your tongue. Filling your heart with right thinking and perspective will protect you from allowing bad things to spill out of your mouth. I once heard a preacher say, "If you want to know what a man is full of, just bump him really hard. Once he is unsettled, whatever sloshes out is what he has always been full of." That is exactly what Jesus is saying in Luke 6, and it is also what the apostle James is teaching us in today's verses.

So, in order to begin to bring these things under control, let me suggest two areas where we need to gain control.

1. Perspective

When we see things correctly, we tend to be able to react to them correctly. In order for us to have a right perspective on the world around us, we must realize a few things.

First of all, we must remember that each and every one of us is created in the image of God. The apostle clearly points this out when he says we are human beings "who have been made in God's likeness." This means that you are made in the likeness of God. Therefore, everything you do reflects on the God in whose image you have been made. With that thought in mind, ask yourself some questions:

- What should flow out of the mouth of someone made in the image of God?
- What thoughts should be allowed to exist in the mind of someone made in the image of God?
- What words or thoughts have no place in the mind and mouth of someone made in the image of God?

Secondly, the apostle is reminding us that everyone around us is made in the image of God. People we like, and people we don't like, are all made in the image of God. People living up to God's image in them, and people not living up to that image, are all created in the image of God. It is that *imago Dei* (image of God) that we must learn to see and to respect in people. The very fact that they are created in the image of God gives them value that exists regardless of how we may feel about how they act or what they do. With that thought in mind, ask yourself some more questions:

- What should I be saying about someone who is made in the image of God?
- What should I not be saying about someone who is made in the image of God?

That person I don't like, (insert name here), has been made in the image of God, so knowing that, how should I change the way I think or feel or act toward him or her?

2. Exposure

It is really difficult to see things from the proper perspective when you are surrounded by improper thoughts, feelings, actions, and ideas. It's tough to be an eagle when turkeys surround you!

So, control your surroundings.

We must learn to gain control of everything that enters our minds and our hearts. That means we must control, to the best of our ability, the environment to which we allow ourselves to be exposed. When you are constantly bombarded with unhealthy images, messages, words, ideas, sounds, and emotions, you will never be able to maintain a healthy perspective. Therefore, you will never be able to maintain a healthy and clean heart. Therefore, you will never be able to develop and maintain a healthy and clean mouth. Now with that thought in mind, ask yourself a few more questions:

- Which negative influences am I allowing to feed into my life and mind?
- How about the media I allow into my life? Is it healthy? Wholesome?
- How about the people around me? Are they healthy? Wholesome? Kind?

Actually, the apostle Paul gives us a great checklist that is extremely helpful in situations like this one: "Finally, brothers and sisters, whatever is true, whatever is noble, whatever is right, whatever is pure, whatever is lovely, whatever is admirable—if anything is excellent or praiseworthy—think about such things" (Phil. 4:8).

19

Who is wise and understanding among you? Let them show it by their good life, by deeds done in the humility that comes from wisdom.

—James 3:13

The Greek word here translated as "good life" is the word *anastrophe*. This word is translated in the King James Version as "a good conversation" and in the New American Standard Bible as "good behavior." I find it interesting that these three translators would use such different words to translate this one word to English. However, the actual definition of the Greek word is "behavior—conversation."[1] So, let's consider what we might glean from this rather dual-defined word.

Our behavior is the conversation of our lives. A good man does not need to trumpet the good things he has done his entire life. A woman who has helped and uplifted people does not need to remind people of how much she helped them and lifted them up. People remember that kind of thing.

Your life is your conversation. If you are trying to change the conversation, that says more about you than it does about anyone else.

I love spending time with older saints, especially pastors. I love to listen to the stories they tell of God's faithfulness and blessing in their lives. When I was in college, we had a professor who some students really didn't like too much. He constantly told stories—from his days as a pastor, a student, and a college professor. He just liked telling stories. I loved his class. While I may have learned less book knowledge from him than more traditional professors, I learned more about life and ministry from him than any other professor in my entire time in college. It was the reliving of the accounts of God's goodness and faithfulness that taught me one of the most valuable lessons I could have ever learned.

I can trust God—always.

My grandfathers were like this too. They would sit and talk to me about how God had blessed, sustained, or guided them and how other people had helped or hindered God's plan for their lives. All the while, I was hearing what I think the Holy Spirit wanted me to hear. I was hearing the conversation of a life lived well. I want to be like that one day. I want to tell the story of my life to my children and grandchildren and have them hear the goodness and faithfulness of God as I talk. I want them to see that they can trust God because "if he never failed Grandpa, he will never fail me." I want to talk about my life and my God in such a way that God gets all the glory for his strength and faithfulness, and I am remembered only as having followed well. Then, the words of my mouth and the joy of my heart will be a true blessing because of the surrender of my life to the Savior of my soul!

20

But if you harbor bitter envy and selfish ambition in your hearts, do not boast about it or deny the truth. Such "wisdom" does not come down from heaven but is earthly, unspiritual, demonic.

—James 3:14–15

So, have you watched much media or television lately? Bitter envy and selfish ambition could define the plot lines of virtually every reality TV show, and many, if not most of the series that we watch on a daily basis. As a culture, we are entertained by bitter envy and selfish ambition.

Nervous yet? You should be.

These emotions are core to who we are. This is clear in Genesis when Cain killed Abel. The issue was Cain's bitter envy toward Abel and his relationship with God. It was Cain's own selfish ambition. He must have believed that once Abel was out of the way, God would be forced to love and honor Cain. This same bitterness, selfishness, and envy are still with us today. It is unchecked, unbridled, uninhibited, and too often celebrated. We absolutely love it when athletes forget humility and declare they are the best that has ever been. We rush out to buy music, movies, and videos from artists who boldly proclaim to be the "god" of a particular genre of music or art. We get tattoos to carry their words with us forever. We buy athletic jerseys and wear their names on our backs. We celebrate their bitter envy and selfish ambition, and we do so to our own detriment.

God clearly warns against this kind of behavior. The apostle James says that such thinking is not from God, but is unspiritual and demonic! Wow, that should cause you to pause! Truth is, we really do celebrate these destructive emotions that Scripture calls demonic. We truly reap the very harvest that the apostle tells us we are going to see.

"Disorder and every evil practice" is a vivid description of much of our culture today (v. 16). When people do not get their own way, they seem to become immediately disorderly and destructive. They demand that their own selfish ambition be fed and celebrated, and if it is not, then they take it out on whomever they choose to blame for their own failure. Then society celebrates their actions and encourages more of the same from other people.

When selfishness is celebrated, what outcome would you expect? I find it almost laughable, if it weren't so incredibly sad and destructive, that as a culture we celebrate selfishness and then seem confused when there is a lack of selflessness in our culture. Well, what did you expect? If our heroes are filled with envy and selfish ambition, do we really believe that we are encouraging selfless behavior? No. As with everything else, what we celebrate, we duplicate. So when we celebrate envy and selfish ambition, we duplicate envy and selfish ambition. Once the entire culture is driven by its own envy and selfish ambition, then the only possible outcome is "disorder and every evil practice."

So, let me encourage you to do two things:

- Be a person of selfless service.
- Celebrate people of selfless service.

What we celebrate, we can duplicate!

21

But the wisdom that comes from heaven is first of all pure; then peace-loving, considerate, submissive, full of mercy and good fruit, impartial and sincere.

—James 3:17

Now that we have looked at what the world celebrates and found it to be dangerous and destructive, the question becomes, what should we celebrate and therefore attempt to duplicate in our lives? And the apostle does not disappoint!

The list James gives here in this verse is a clear description of what heaven-born wisdom looks like.

It "is first of all pure." The Greek word, *hagnos*, indicates that this word should perhaps be interpreted as "certain" or "sure."[1] Therefore, what we should hear when we read these words is: "The wisdom that comes from heaven is certain and sure." This clearly shows that what we are about to read from the apostle is trustworthy.

It is "peace-loving." This is certainly contrary to what is celebrated in our culture. Even in our news programming, we are fed a constant stream of stories of uproars and violence, arguments and fights. However, the wisdom of heaven is to love peace, not argument. This is sometimes a lesson lost even on the church! I have run into far too many argumentative and angry Christians, pastors, and churches. These so-called followers of Christ have certainly missed this description of the wisdom of heaven!

It is "considerate." The Greek word is *epieikes*, and it is defined as "appropriate, mild; gentle; patient."[2] Again, this is directly the opposite of what our society seems to celebrate. Being considerate is not expected in our culture. Working hard to get your own way is the expected norm.

It is "submissive." The word here is defined as "easily obeying, compliant."[3] Once again, this is not a trait that is celebrated in our culture. However, if one is following truth, compliance is absolutely the best strategy. If one is following anything other than truth, shouldn't that person double-check why they are following what they are following? In other words, perhaps obedience would make more sense if we were following the wisdom of heaven instead of the wisdom of demons (James 3:15).

It is "full of mercy and good fruit." The idea here is that one is showing kindness and producing good works and good deeds. Simply put, by showing kindness and forgiveness to the people around us, we produce good things in, around, and through our lives. Our mercy produces good fruit.

It is "impartial and sincere." The meaning is "without partiality" and "without hypocrisy." You see, far too often we get so committed to our own version of truth that we refuse to hear anyone else's version, even God's. Once we find ourselves in that place, we press back against anyone and anything that challenges our view of things. In fact, it can become so bad that we can actually realize that we are wrong and still refuse to admit it. We can actually find ourselves arguing in defense of something we know is incorrect. When that happens, our partiality (stubbornness) gives birth to hypocrisy (not believing or living out what we say we believe). It is a sad thing but that describes far too many Christians. When we allow our thinking to be impartial and not blocked by our own stubborn ideas, we can actually find truth and live out what is right.

Peacemakers who sow in peace reap a harvest of righteousness.
—James 3:18

I once heard someone compare peacemakers and peacekeepers. *Peacekeepers* are not there to bring correction or healing. That is not their job. Peacekeepers are really only there to maintain the status quo. Obviously, though, the status quo isn't working or there would be no need for peacekeepers. *Peacemakers* are another breed altogether. These folks are not interested in maintaining a broken status quo. In fact, they are looking for right ideas, right directions, right solutions, and right people. They will anger some folks, and they will cause some trouble, but they will make peace in the end. The making of peace allows the establishment of righteousness.

PART 4

JAMES 4

22

What causes fights and quarrels among you? Don't they come from your desires that battle within you? You desire but do not have, so you kill. You covet but you cannot get what you want, so you quarrel and fight.

—James 4:1–2

What an incredibly descriptive phrase the apostle uses here, and it is absolutely correct. It would be rather easy for me to take you on a journey through history, or even current events, and show you how this truth plays out on a global scale. We can clearly see how the "desires" and "covetousness" of a Hitler wrought mass destruction across all of Europe during World War II. We can see the same thing play out in dictator after dictator: Stalin, Lenin, Pol Pot, Mao Zedong, and others like them. It is obvious in these cases how self-centered desires and covetousness, left unchecked, can cause great destruction.

What about the same self-centeredness, covetousness, and lust on a much smaller scale? What about the same unchecked sinfulness in your life, my life, or the life of my neighbor? Honestly, the results are just as personally devastating. Death and destruction will follow selfishness, lust, and covetousness every time. We must work diligently to extract these, by the blood of Jesus and the power of the Holy Spirit, from our lives. If we don't, they will destroy us.

Now, you may be thinking that I am being a bit overly dramatic here, but I am not. As James wrote to these first-century Christians, he likely wrote to churches that had experienced murder and robbery caused by the ambitious desire of one person in the congregation to have the things or position of another. He likely wrote to a group who had witnessed firsthand the destructive nature of these sins. And he wrote to them in such a way as to help them understand the root cause of this behavior.

You see, some would say, "Well, just stop stealing, or cheating, or killing, and everything will be alright." It's not that simple. The stealing, cheating, and killing are not the real problems; they are simply symptoms of the problem. J. Vernon McGee gives an account that describes this dilemma well: "A brother of Henry Ward Beecher, a pastor in upper New York state, had a clock in his church that never would keep accurate time. So this man put a sign under that clock which read: 'Don't blame the hands. The trouble lies deeper.'"[1]

And so it is with the sins we commit. The real trouble is not in our hands; the real trouble is in our hearts.

We enter arguments and refuse to settle them because of our own evil desires that battle within us. We have affairs and take someone else's spouse because of our own evil desires that battle within us. We cheat on our taxes because of our own evil desires that battle within us. We steal from our workplace because of our own evil desires that battle within us. We enter into physical fights because of our own evil desires that battle within us. We drink and party, destroying our credibility and health, because of our own evil desires that battle within us. While we try and blame the marriage, the alcohol, the drug, the boss, the system, the bully, or the parents who raised us, the truth is much simpler: Our own evil desires battle within us.

So, what must change are the desires that exist within us. We must begin the process of having our own desires changed. I have often said in sermons and conversations that you cannot change your heart by changing your actions; you must change your actions by changing your heart. When your "want to" changes, your "will do" follows. Simply put, people do what they want to do. So if you want to change what you do, you must do the work of changing what you want to do. Sound easy (see Rom. 7:15–25)?

Now, I am not going to play games here. This is going to be tough work. This is going to be long-term work. The process of changing desires and changing the heart can take a lifetime. All along the way there are improvements, betterments, and noticeable changes that others see, and you see. As these changes take hold, they begin to build a momentum of their own and that momentum helps you journey on from tough change to tough change without losing hope or energy. The process is long but it is worth it. Think about it: The alternative is that we destroy our lives and perhaps the lives of others around us because of our own evil desires that battle within us.

23

You do not have because you do not ask God. When you ask, you do not receive, because you ask with wrong motives, that you may spend what you get on your pleasures.

—James 4:2–3

Again, the apostle knocks on the door of our hearts and calls us to a very real change in the way we think and process our own desires. He now takes us a level deeper into the damage that wrong desires can have in our lives. He clearly attaches a failed prayer life to the desires of our hearts. I think we can best understand this from two potential points of view.

Some people are so deeply disconnected from God that they truly do not even consider asking him for guidance or provision when they have needs. They have convinced themselves that there is no need to even bother asking. These folks fall into a few categories.

1. God isn't even there.

Some people have convinced themselves that God just doesn't exist. It would be futile to call out to a God who does not exist. So for these folks, there is a desperation that is caused by a lack of purpose, direction, and meaning. This is true simply because, if there is no Designer to the universe, then there is no design. If there is no design, then there is no purpose. If there is no purpose, then there is no meaning. For these folks, the change in thinking must begin with the realization that there is a God who designed everything and has a plan for every life.

2. God doesn't even care.

Some folks believe there is a God, but they are not convinced that he is a good, caring, loving God. For them, God is simply a cosmic force or ruler in the sky who randomly looks down for his own entertainment. Once in a while, he may choose for whatever reason to cause something to occur in this world, but that is usually not good news. God is just disinterested. For these folks, the change in thinking must begin with the realization that God is good and that he actually cares. He is listening, and he is willing to help.

3. God won't hear me.

Finally, there are those who are just convinced that they have been so bad that God would never want anything to do with them. If this is how you feel, then remember the account of Jesus' death on the cross (see Luke 23:39–43). The thief who hung on the cross next to him asked him for mercy, and Jesus gave it! This man had not lived a good life. In fact, his sins had been so terrible that they had earned him the death penalty.

Further, there was no time for him to make things right. He was going to be dead before the sun went down. Even with his terrible history, his horrible sin, and his complete lack of opportunity to make things right, Jesus forgave him. If Jesus will hear and forgive that man, then he will certainly hear and forgive you!

When you ask, you do not receive, because you ask with wrong motives, that you may spend what you get on your pleasures.

—James 4:3

Some people are actually connected with God and deeply believe in him. These folks talk with God daily and ask God about and for everything they need, and yet sometimes they seem to hear nothing from him. So the question arises, "What am I doing wrong?"

The answer to that question may be really simple: check your motives. Sometimes we fail to have our prayers answered because of our own evil desires that battle within us. As they battle within us, they drive us to ask for things that we do not need and would not use wisely. Always remember that God is an excellent manager of resources. If he knows that you will poorly manage something that you have asked for, or even that you would use it in a way that would bring harm to you and those around you, he may not answer that prayer.

And you should be glad if he doesn't! Sometimes our greatest praise should be reserved for unanswered prayers! God knows and desires what is best for us. If we are ever going to get on the same page with him, we are going to have to change what motivates us.

24

You adulterous people, don't you know that friendship with the world means enmity against God? Therefore, anyone who chooses to be a friend of the world becomes an enemy of God. Or do you think Scripture says without reason that he jealously longs for the spirit he has caused to dwell in us?

—James 4:4–5

Let's break this next verse down one piece at a time.

"You adulterous people." This phrase is really strong. The idea here is one that is repeated many times in the Old Testament and then is brought into the New Testament by the Jewish apostles. In fact, *adulterous* and variations of the term are used seven times in the New Testament. Jesus used it three times (see Matt. 12:39; Matt. 16:4; Mark 8:38), the apostle Paul used it once (see Rom. 7:3), James used it twice here in chapter 4, and Peter used it once (see 2 Pet. 2:14). The idea is harsh and can be rather insulting in today's cultural context. However, it clearly communicates. In the Old Testament when the Israelites would give up worshiping their God for the worship of other gods, God and his prophets would compare them to adulterous women who refused to remain true to their husbands. Just like those women who would abandon their faithful husbands and run from bed to bed seeking some new thrill, the people of God were abandoning their faithful God in search of some new spiritual thrill.

Today is no different. While we would not isolate the example to adulterous women but instead include adulterous men in the equation, the lesson is no less clear. When we abandon the God who has been faithful to us for some other form of religion or philosophy, we are like adulterous spouses who simply refuse to remain true to the One who loves us unconditionally.

"Don't you know that friendship with the world means enmity against God? therefore, anyone who chooses to be a friend of the world becomes an enemy of God. Or do you think Scripture says without reason that he jealously longs for the spirit he has caused to dwell in us?" Let's stay with the adultery analogy for just a moment. Over my years of life and ministry, I have run into many different marriages and different people. From time to time, I run into a situation when one spouse simply cannot understand why they cannot remain married and have their stable life at home while still running around and sleeping around on their partner. We even have a name for it these days: an open marriage. Let me be completely clear that there is nothing open about the commitment two people make to each other when they get married. The idea that *anyone* should be okay with their spouse sleeping around and then coming home to them once they have had their fill of someone else is repulsive. It just isn't fair. That cheating spouse expects to be allowed to run amok and still find the one they promised to be with for life waiting faithfully at home with open, loving arms. Ridiculous. (There are other words in my head but the last chapter of James taught me to control my tongue!)

This is exactly what we do to God when we come home to him on Sunday but then mess around with sins, addictions, habits, religions, gods, and philosophies of the world Monday through Saturday. We are spiritual adulterers.

I don't know why, but God always gives more grace (v. 6). God is so much better than any one of us. Most of us, if not all, would have long since rejected the "Christian" people of this world. We have cheated on God endlessly, and yet he still forgives. The great message of Christ is that God always forgives. There is more grace in God than we could ever begin to imagine, understand, or explain. And just when we are convinced that we have finally gone too far, and this must be the end of God's grace for us, we discover that we are wrong. If we simply humble ourselves before him, his grace sets us free.

Now, we cannot allow our pride to block us from asking for forgiveness! All too often we do just that. We arrogantly declare: "There is nothing wrong with what I just did!" With that declaration, we stand in defiance of God's holiness and refuse to humble ourselves in order to experience his grace. What an incredible mistake. God desires to forgive, but our own pride can keep us from finding that forgiveness.

25

Submit yourselves, then, to God.
Resist the devil, and he will flee from you.
—James 4:7

The thought continues. We find forgiveness and freedom by submitting ourselves to a God who shows grace at levels we simply cannot comprehend. You know, people really hate that word *submit.* So let's be realistic about this. Everyone is going to submit to something. We are all actively submitting either to a system of thinking, an addiction, a goal, a vision, an authority, or a person. The truth of grace is that we can choose to submit to a God whose goal is to forgive us and make our lives better. When you find a God like that, submission can actually become a joy and not a burden.

If we resist the devil, he will flee from us. This is good news! Too many people think that their sin is inevitable. In fact, we have given up on fighting against the sin in our lives to the point that we have begun to define ourselves by our sin. We will say things like, "I am an alcoholic," or "I am an addict," or "I am (choose your sin and insert here)." The reality is nothing like that.

I am a child of God!

Nothing more, but nothing less! As a child of God, I do not have to be any of those other things. The word *resist* is really quite vivid. The Greek word *anthistemi* is translated here as: "To set oneself against; to stand against; to oppose; resist."[1] So rather than giving in to our sin, or in other words giving in to Satan, perhaps we should *stand against* our sin. Perhaps we should set ourselves against our sin. Perhaps we should actually oppose that to which we once surrendered. The apostle tells us that if we do, Satan will flee.

Come near to God and he will come near to you. Wash your hands, you sinners, and purify your hearts, you double-minded.

—James 4:8

There is more to this than just standing against and resisting temptation. Remember, you cannot change your heart by changing your actions. You must change your actions by changing your heart. If you resist the devil, he will flee from you. If you draw near to God, he will draw near to you. When you draw near to God, you naturally drive away Satan. The more time you spend drawing near to God, the more you will find your hands clean and your heart focused. It's not really complicated; whatever you allow around you will eventually get in you and will eventually define you. So if you are a "spiritual adulterer" and spend much of your time around people, actions, and philosophies that oppose God, those things will eventually define you. If you remain committed to God and draw near to him, then he will ultimately define you.

And I promise you that his ways have a much better outcome!

James 4:9 seems like an odd passage but it actually teaches a profound truth. Sin should cause us to "grieve, mourn and wail." Far too often today, we simply make light of sinful behavior. It doesn't shock us to see people act in a sinful way, and it doesn't grieve us. In this change in attitude toward sin, even within the church, we start to see callousness toward sinfulness. In this callousness, we fail to recognize the depth of harm we do to ourselves, our families, our communities, and to the very heart of God, when we act in sinful ways. It is true that if you humble yourself, God "will lift you up." That does not negate the harm done by sin, and that harm should break our hearts. It certainly breaks the heart of God.

So go ahead and grieve, mourn, wail, be sad and sorry for all the sin in your life.

Then humble yourself before God and receive the joyous truth of his grace.

26

Brothers and sisters, do not slander one another. Anyone who speaks against a brother or sister or judges them speaks against the law and judges it. When you judge the law, you are not keeping it, but sitting in judgment on it. There is only one Lawgiver and Judge, the one who is able to save and destroy. But you—who are you to judge your neighbor?

—James 4:11–12

Now here is some good advice for church people. I am not sure why this is, but church folks seem to take great joy in talking bad about one another. It is almost like we view it as important to show the rest of the world that we don't agree or that we find some other group or person somehow spiritually repulsive. In this really odd feeding frenzy of bitterness and negativity, innocent people get hurt, and seeking people get disillusioned. I have actually sat and talked with pastors who refuse to talk with other pastors whom they have never met simply because they hold different doctrinal positions on some obscure point. I am convinced that if they got together, they would like one another, but they won't even talk to each other, because they are so busy disagreeing with one another from a distance.

Once I had a parishioner come to me after church very upset. He said, "I went to so and so church last Sunday, and the sermon seemed to be about you! The pastor kept saying bad things about you. I know those things aren't true, and I almost stood up and corrected him. Should I do something about this?" I assured him that this wasn't the first time that something like this had happened, and then I let him in on a little secret. It doesn't matter much what that preacher thinks of me, because he isn't my judge. I told him like I have told others: If that pastor can get good mileage in his congregation by bashing a man he has never met, then leave him alone. As long as he is preaching the gospel once in a while, he can bash me all he wants. It's a waste of his time, and it puts him at odds with the apostle James in this passage of Scripture, but leave him alone, and God will judge me and him both. Now, while that was my take in this particular instance, don't let it give you *permission* to slander me or any other brother or sister in Christ. The apostle here makes it abundantly clear that this is not acceptable behavior.

Consider what you are really doing when you slander a brother or sister in Christ. You are looking at their lives and God's law, and in between those two things, you are inserting your opinion. In other words, you are declaring, by your own words and actions, that you are the arbiter of the meaning of God's law. You are suggesting that if there were a "Scriptural Supreme Court," you should have a seat on that court as judge. You would take the authority of God's law and apply it based on your interpretation in such a way that your brothers and sisters in Christ are bound to think like you.

That doesn't sound like the freedom of grace that the apostle Paul talks about. That doesn't sound like the forgiveness and grace that every New Testament writer talks about. That just doesn't sound much like Christ at all. In fact, that sounds a lot like the Pharisees, and Jesus didn't speak too highly of them.

This is where my angst comes in with this type of judgmentalism within the church. When we set ourselves up as the final arbiter or judge of what God's Word demands or means, we become modern-day Pharisees. We demand that everyone else read and understand Scripture *exactly* like we do. We demand that they act like us, think like us, dress like us, worship like us, and talk like us.

The beauty of Jesus is that he accepted people right where they were. Then he brought them toward righteousness in their own time and manner, so that their relationship with Christ did not require some unnatural uniformity that is not achievable among human beings. When we try to force that kind of unnatural uniformity, we forget that it is Jesus, and Jesus alone, who is the ultimate judge of each and every one of us.

By the way, Jesus was not a Catholic, Protestant, Baptist, Methodist, Wesleyan, Pentecostal, or charismatic. Jesus was—and is—the very Son of God sent to bring forgiveness and healing to *all* humankind, even the ones who don't think like I do! That's awesome!

27

Now listen, you who say, "Today or tomorrow we will go to this or that city, spend a year there, carry on business and make money." Why, you do not even know what will happen tomorrow. What is your life? You are a mist that appears for a little while and then vanishes.

—James 4:13–14

I am a huge advocate of planning ahead. In fact, I often talk with those around me in ministry and in life about end-game thinking. I want to consider all the possible outcomes of any given possible decision and think those outcomes through as far out as possible. When I do this, I am able to consider, and often avoid, unintended consequences. Most every choice has some unintended and unforeseen consequences. So, as I write this, I am not advocating any lack of planning.

However, the truth is that none of us really know what tomorrow holds. In fact, none of us has any guarantee that we will even be here tomorrow. Our tomorrows are not in our hands; they are firmly in the hands of God. Therefore, we should be careful how we think.

These verses from the apostle are not a restriction against planning. They are more a perspective check. When we make plans and fail to consider the temporary nature of our own existence, we begin to think like we will always be here. And that just isn't true. When we begin to function as if we will always be here, we forget that the only one who is always around is God himself. When we forget that, we run the very real risk of acting and planning as if we are God, which we are not. Therefore, we should put a natural pause in our thinking and planning.

Here is the plan: Always put room for God in your planning. When we add the phrase "if it is the Lord's will" to our planning, we acknowledge his sovereignty (v. 15). We are reminded that God is in charge, and we are not. Now listen, this phrase is not for God's benefit; it is for ours. Sometimes people seem to think they need to say certain things in certain ways for *God's* benefit. Well, that just isn't true. God doesn't need anything from us. We can't do anything for his benefit. When we remind ourselves that God is in control, we are doing ourselves a favor and reminding ourselves that we are not in control. That is a great reality check!

James 4:16 says for a person to boast arrogantly is evil. And here is the end of the matter. Those who refuse to leave room in their planning for God and his will are acting out of arrogance. They are insisting that they know what is best, when is best, how is best, and who is best. When in reality, only God knows all of those things.

Everyone eventually gets over this type of arrogance. When confronted with our own mortality, through injury, sickness, or age, we tend to come to grips with who God really is and who is in control. We tend to understand, in the end, that we will do this or that and go here or there only "if it is the Lord's will."

28

If anyone, then, knows the good they ought to do and doesn't do it, it is sin for them.
—James 4:17

I believe that sin is a willful transgression of a known law of God. By this, I mean that sin is something that we do on purpose. It is, in the end, willful disobedience to what we know God has called us to do or not to do. This willful disobedience results in sinful behaviors. One would be hard pressed to find an example in Scripture of sin that God punished that was anything but a willful transgression of a known law. In other words, I don't see God punishing people for things they did not know were wrong.

With that thought in mind, consider the verse we are dealing with: "If anyone" (including you and me) "knows the good they ought to do" (have been enlightened to what God desires for us to accomplish) "and doesn't do it" (knowingly choosing by our own free will to not do that which God commanded), "it is sin for them." Well, I can't really say it any clearer than that.

When you know God wants you to do something, just do it! Also, when you know God *doesn't* want you to do something, don't do it! This is how we avoid sin.

Now, let's take this one step further. While many people say that you cannot categorize sin, I think you actually can put it into broad categories. Let's discuss two that relate to what the apostle is teaching us here.

1. Sins of Commission

A *sin of commission* is a sin that I actually commit. When I choose to do something that I know I should not do, I commit sin. These sins are usually very blatant and obvious. There is no doubt of the sinfulness of the actions in question. It is clear that a sin has been committed. Case closed.

2. Sins of Omission

A *sin of omission* is more complicated. These sins are less obvious and visible. When you omit something God commanded you to do, you simply do nothing. Therefore, it can seem to the rest of the world or the rest of the church that you have no sin in your life at all. It can seem as if you are following God's call faithfully. However, all the while, in the depths of your soul, you know that you are not doing what God has clearly commanded you to do. By choosing to omit that command from your thinking and actions, you have sinned. Even if others can't see it and you can plausibly deny it, you have sinned. Case closed.

Hear the verse again: "If anyone, then, knows the good they ought to do and doesn't do it, it is sin for them." Take that warning seriously, and don't *commit* or *omit* anything that results in sin.

PART 5

JAMES 5

29

Now listen, you rich people, weep and wail because of the misery that is coming on you. Your wealth has rotted, and moths have eaten your clothes. Your gold and silver are corroded. Their corrosion will testify against you and eat your flesh like fire. You have hoarded wealth in the last days. Look! The wages you failed to pay the workers who mowed your fields are crying out against you. The cries of the harvesters have reached the ears of the Lord Almighty. You have lived on earth in luxury and self-indulgence. You have fattened yourselves in the day of slaughter. You have condemned and murdered the innocent one, who was not opposing you.

—James 5:1–6

On an initial reading of this passage of Scripture, one might conclude that it is not a good thing to be rich. You might even decide that God does not like rich people. But none of that is true. The Bible never condemns wealth. In fact, wealthy people are numbered among the followers of Christ, even among the disciples. Wealthy people are celebrated as examples to be followed throughout the Old Testament. The Bible just does not condemn wealth. People look at verses like this one and rail against anyone who has more than they do. In the end, that is how we typically describe the *wealthy*—people who have what I wish I had. All too often, that causes the one who has less to covet, and coveting itself is sin.

No, what the apostle is actually speaking to here is greed, unkindness, and hoarding. The problem is not that some people have more than others. That always has been true, and quite frankly, it always will be true. The problem is that some people who have more refuse to dispense any of it to others. They are selfish hoarders of wealth who really have no care or concern for their fellow man. God does not approve of that behavior. He does not like it when people hoard their wealth while their neighbors starve. He does not like it when people underpay or refuse to pay workers just to save a dollar. He does not like it when people cheat and steal in order to take from the poor and enrich themselves. Such people will find very little comfort from God on the day of judgment.

While I was working my way through college, I took a job selling pots and pans. As I write this, I am still using that cookware that I earned by selling to others almost thirty years ago. Those are good pots and pans! However, they were terribly expensive. After doing this for a little while, I was completely convinced of the quality and worth of the product, but I began to notice something that I did not like. I was a capable salesman, and many of my customers would buy the product. I found myself selling really expensive pots and pans to folks I knew could hardly pay their rent. They would put this cookware on layaway and sign a contract that clearly stated that if they failed to make the layaway payments, they would not get the cookware, *and* they would lose their money. I knew what would happen, and I just couldn't keep doing it. I was earning my commission, but they were going to lose their money. I had to quit, and I did. For me, money was not important enough to cause pain and financial loss to others. I couldn't see past them and their needs in order to make my money and fulfill my own needs. And that is how I think God wants us to view the world.

The problem is not having money. The problem is having money at the expense of others. The problem is refusing to use the money you have to enhance and improve the lives of others around you.

It is interesting to note that as the apostle James wrote these words, and as Jesus taught his lessons to the wealthy, they spoke into a culture that did not have a middle class. There was the very wealthy class and then the very poor. As Jesus and James saw the suffering of the poor and opulence of the rich, they commanded the rich to be kind to the poor. They warned that if kindness was not shown, judgment would come from God. Perhaps as little as ten years would pass between James sending out this letter to the church and the complete destruction of Jerusalem by the Roman general, Titus, in AD 70. The descriptions of the siege and ultimate fall of Jerusalem make the apostle's word here fully prophetic.

While we live in a modern culture with a healthy middle class today, we tend to lose sight of the fact that James was speaking directly to us. Remember, *wealthy* can be defined as someone who has more than I do. By that math, almost all Americans are wealthy in someone's eyes. Therefore, we must take heed of what the apostle wrote here. God will judge us one day on how well we managed the resources he gave to us. I don't know about you, but I want him to look at me and see kindness and generosity.

30

Be patient, then, brothers and sisters, until the Lord's coming. See how the farmer waits for the land to yield its valuable crop, patiently waiting for the autumn and spring rains. You too, be patient and stand firm, because the Lord's coming is near.

—James 5:7–8

Let's put these two verses up against the first six verses we read in this chapter and get a fuller view of what the apostle was really saying to us. The first six verses contain an admonition to the wealthy, warning them of the judgment to come if they do not learn to be kind, generous, and fair in their dealings and their business. Then, here in verse 7, we find the apostle telling his brothers and sisters to "be patient." This begs the question, patient for what? The Lord's coming!

The apostle reminds those who are in the church that Jesus will return. When he does return, he will make all the wrong things right and all the unfair things fair. Jesus will fix everything. The word translated here into "the Lord's coming" is the Greek word *parousia*. This word is better known to us in its Latin form, *advent*. It is directly defined as being near; coming; presence; and return specifically of Christ to punish Jerusalem, or finally the wicked.[1] The message the apostle was sending to these Christians, who were predominantly poor and powerless in a two-tiered system, was to be patient, since Jesus will return and make it all right.

This is our hope even today. The Judeo-Christian base of our current culture makes this one of the best cultures in which to live in all of history. We are historically wealthy, healthy, safe, and free. Even so, there are systems that are designed to ensnare the poor and keep them in poverty. There are wicked people who would take from the poor in order to enrich themselves. There are governments who would steal from the very people they exist to serve, just to line the pockets of their friends and family. Sometimes we can get disillusioned. We can quickly find ourselves questioning God: Why do you allow evil people to prosper? Why do good people sometimes work so hard for so little? How can that guy who cheats do better than the other guy who doesn't?

God calls us to patience. These things have always been true. The sin nature inside of every human being causes this type of mistreatment and evil in our culture and world. God is not turning a blind eye. Every action. Every evil. Every theft. Every murder. Every rape. Every act of unkindness and hard-heartedness is being recorded. There will be a day of judgment.

This judgment is coming. The realization that it is coming affects different people in different ways. To the wealthy mentioned in verses 1–6 of this chapter, there is dread, if not fear, of such a judgment. It is no surprise to me that many of the uncaring wealthy do not believe in any god whatsoever, and especially not the God of the Bible. Why would they willingly choose to give praise to God who has already promised to punish their wickedness? So they rationalize away the very idea of God.

The idea of judgment is peaceful, redemptive, and validating for those who are working hard to live right. The idea that one day the final judge of all things, God himself, will gather all of mankind together, and from his heavenly throne, declare reward and punishment in exact measure, brings joy. The evil will pay for what they have done. Amen! The righteous will be rewarded for what they have done. Amen! The final judgment will be right, because God, the only one who knows the heart and soul of every human being, will be the judge on the throne.

"But Pastor, I have not been such a good person in my life. I think I may be on the wrong side of that judgment event! What can I do?" Ah, my friend, this is where the blood of Jesus comes into sharp focus. He paid a price that I could not pay to win a prize that I do not deserve. He did the same for you. Simply take the time to speak to God and do three simple things:

- **Admit** that you have sinned and need his forgiveness.
- **Believe** that Jesus can and will forgive your sins.
- **Commit** to change your ways to his ways so your life can be better from here forward.

Once that prayer is prayed from a truly sincere heart, this judgment is nothing to be feared. It is something to be anticipated patiently.

Don't grumble against one another, brothers and sisters, or you will be judged. The Judge is standing at the door!
—James 5:9

I suppose that grumbling against one another within the church family is one of the greatest detriments to the spread of the gospel. Think of all the time we waste arguing amongst ourselves. Baptists argue with Pentecostals. Methodists argue with Lutherans. Catholics argue with Protestants. Calvinists argue with Arminians. Independent nondenominationalists argue with those in denominations. Fundamentalists argue with . . . well, you get the point. And all the while, Satan is thrilled.

Honestly, as long as we are arguing with each other, the devil can just take a vacation. He and his minions no doubt are fueling these arguments. It has gotten so bad that the best minds in all of Christianity are not out trying to find ways to win the world for Christ; instead, they are holed up in some dusty office in some old university building trying to find ways to defend their tribe from another one—and all of this among Christians!

Here I am speaking only of the broader church, but the same garbage happens in local churches. The women's ministry argues with the men's ministry. The children's ministry argues with the youth ministry. The decorating committee argues with the building committee. The pastor argues with the board—and on and on it goes.

It is a brilliant strategy. Our enemy divides us against each other and thereby keeps us focused on anything other than the goal in front of us, which is reaching the lost! As long as we are fighting over petty things, we cannot be focused on important things. I have seen so many churches destroyed by a grumbling spirit. Once that spirit of grumbling takes hold in a group of people, it is almost impossible to root out. One person with a grumbling spirit can ruin an entire church, if they are not dealt with right away. Likewise, one person with a grumbling spirit can ruin an entire family vacation, an entire family event, or an entire family.

We must internally fight against the grumbling spirit that desires to overtake us. We must gently deal with the grumblers that have taken up residence around us. Let me suggest a few ways to deal with both.

1. Prayer

Whether you are dealing with someone else or a grumbling spirit threatens to rise up inside of you, always begin with prayer. Soon, in just a few verses, we are going to have an extended conversation about the power of prayer. Let me simply say that it is difficult to *be* a grumbler or to be *mean* to a grumbler, when you are praying about a grumbling spirit. Prayer changes things—by changing me.

2. Kindness

Grumbling is one of those beasts that is best killed with kindness. Through the many years I have dealt with people, I have found that when I confront grumblers head on, and do so with kindness, they almost always back down. Even if they don't, they find the need to move on. By dealing with grumblers with kindness, you avoid any stigma that might attach to you. If you yell at them or mistreat them, you validate their grumbling and become equally guilty of causing division. When you kill the grumbling beast with kindness, you play no part in the devil's scheme.

3. Environment

Make every attempt to create an environment that is not conducive to grumbling. In other words, don't do or set up things that you know are going to unnecessarily tick people off, especially those who are grumpy. Now, that does not mean that you let them run the show! It just means that you take everyone's feelings into account when you make plans. If you focus on prayer and kindness, you will set the right environment to weaken the spirit of grumbling further.

4. Grace

Grace is huge! It must remain huge within moments of conflict. When you are facing a grumbler and you come to the place that prayer, kindness, and environment do not seem to be making the situation better, you must have grace to make difficult choices. With kindness, with much prayer, and in the proper place, you may simply need to put distance between yourself and the grumbler.

I have had people challenge me on this thinking before. "Shouldn't you be able to get along with everyone?" "You should never give up on anyone!" "Jesus left the ninety-nine to find the one!" All this is true, but it is in the wrong context here. Yes, we should be able to get along with everyone, but getting along is a two-way street. If someone else is not willing to get along, then sometimes distance brings peace. That distance does not mean you are giving up on them. You must not stop praying for them and showing kindness to them at every opportunity. You just need to bring peace to your environment. Yes, Jesus left the ninety-nine sheep to go find the one in his parable of the lost sheep (see Matt. 18:12–13 and Luke 15:4–6); however, there is no indication of this sheep being a grumbler. No, he wandered off and was helpless, defenseless, and afraid. This is not at all descriptive of your everyday grumbler; therefore, this is not an appropriate comparison. A more appropriate comparison is found just after this parable in Matthew 18. When talking of conflict within the church, Jesus concluded his teaching with these words, "If they still refuse to listen, tell it to the church; and if they refuse to listen even to the church, treat them as you would a pagan or a tax collector" (v. 17).

32

Brothers and sisters, as an example of patience in the face of suffering, take the prophets who spoke in the name of the Lord. As you know, we count as blessed those who have persevered. You have heard of Job's perseverance and have seen what the Lord finally brought about. The Lord is full of compassion and mercy.

—James 5:10–11

Now, in case you were a little put off by yesterday's reading, let's clear something up with today's reading. When Jesus gave us the admonition in Matthew 18:17 to "treat them as you would a pagan or a tax collector," he was saying something rather profound. Think about it. Jesus ran into many tax collectors, and he worked hard at reaching them. Matthew was a tax collector and became one of the disciples. Zacchaeus (see Luke 19:1–10) was a tax collector, and Jesus made a point of having dinner at his house. The apostle Paul ran into pagans on many occasions in Acts, and on every occasion, he worked his hardest to reach them with the gospel. The fact that we would treat someone "as you would a pagan or a tax collector," does not indicate rudeness, unkindness, a lack of concern, or a failure to attempt to redeem his or her relationship to either our Lord or ourselves. It is simply a matter of wise patience.

Patience in the face of adversity is the greatest tool we have to combat the trials we face in life. Victory does not always go to the strongest, the fastest, the smartest, or the most talented. Victory goes to the survivor—the one left standing at the end receives the crown. This should come to us as good news. Most of us are not the strongest, the fastest, the smartest, the most talented, or even the bravest people we know. But we can persevere. And by persevere, I mean choose not to quit!

When we simply hang in there, we are by default winning the battle. Think about that for a moment. God has already won the ultimate war against Satan. He was defeated in heaven and thrown down to the earth, and he was ultimately defeated with the resurrection of Christ on the third day. Therefore, we are already serving the God who wins! So, if we simply endure to the end, we know that we will see victory. Now, I realize that this is not exactly an exciting game plan. "Just hang in there because we win in the end" is not inspiring. However, it is true. The inspiring part is that the Holy Spirit will ultimately give us some level of victory here as we journey on the road to our eternal victory there.

When I was young, I used to go over to help my Grandpa Freeman work in his yard. I still remember those days. Grandpa was not quick, but he was steady. We worked hard, but every so often he would stop and in his slow, determined, deeply southern accent say to me, "Michael, let's stop for a bit." He would then look over to Grandma and say, "Mamma, would you go get me and Michael a Pepsi?" While I was generally a Coke drinker, there was nothing better than an ice-cold Pepsi shared with my grandpa while sitting on a retaining wall on a hot summer day. Get the image. Work to be done. Southern sun beating down. More work than we could possibly accomplish in one day. Aching muscles and tired hands and feet. Best moment ever! So it is with God.

Job gives us just this imagery: a tough life, unbelievable sorrow, inconceivable loss, crushing loneliness, bewildering confusion, and some really bad friends. God sustained him through all of that, and in the end, he looked over at Job and said in that calm, God-like accent: "Job, let's stop for a bit. Holy Spirit, go get Job a new family, some new wealth, a new house, some new clothes, and bring him the best he has ever had. Give him a break so he can rest." More work than could ever get done in a lifetime. More pain than could ever be healed. More questions than could ever be answered. In the midst of it all, a moment with the Master. Best day ever!

33

Above all, my brothers and sisters, do not swear—not by heaven or by earth or by anything else. All you need to say is a simple "Yes" or "No." Otherwise you will be condemned.

—James 5:12

When I was seventeen, I had already graduated from high school and had a full-time job, so I felt the need to do what every young man of that age did: I needed to buy a car! So I went out and looked around. Finally my stepdad came to me and said, "Michael, let's go see Charlie Linker." Well, as it turns out, my dad had always bought his cars from Charlie. So we went over to the car lot where Charlie worked, and sure enough, I found a car there that I absolutely had to have. It was pretty late in the day when we made the decision that I would buy the car, and it was time for Charlie and all the other folks at the dealership to go home. I sat there, a bit disappointed, because I expected that I would have to wait to take my car home. Then Charlie said, "Gray, you and your boy take that car home, and you come back in here whenever you have time and sign the papers." I was a bit stunned by that. It wasn't like we were paying cash; we had to sign a loan for that car. In fact, my dad had to cosign for the car, since I was underage. So my dad looked at Charlie and said, "Don't we need to sign all the loan papers first?" I will never forget

Charlie Linker's response: "Gray Goodman, I wish you owed me a million dollars, because I know if you did, I would see every dime of it come in. Now you and your boy take that car and come sign papers with me whenever you are ready."

I learned a lesson that day. I learned how valuable a reputation is, and I learned how much integrity is really worth. Charlie's opinion of my dad did not appear overnight. It was the result of years of honesty and integrity. Charlie had watched my dad be true to his word time after time until he just trusted him. Trust. That's something that is woefully missing in our current culture. The apostle gives us the recipe for trust: Just let your yes be yes and your no be no.

Trust does not come in the long, wordy sentences of some carefully worded oath. People break their oaths all the time. In fact, the more words there are inside of a given promise, the less likely that the person making the promise intends to keep the promise. The presence of many words indicates a desire to parse meaning and create loopholes. The people you can really trust don't need all those words. They don't need them because they don't intend to ever try and hide behind them. That is what liars do. They make their promises with an overabundance of words. Somewhere in the detail of all those words lies a sneaky little phrase that gives them an out. Then when their promise is no longer convenient, they weasel through that one little phrase that slipped your attention and claim to have never lied since they said that one little thing. "You read the fine print, didn't you? Paragraph nine, section five, subcategory three, line nine? It was clearly there!" That is why there is precious little trust in this world.

We should be different.

Let me tell you a little secret. My dad was not a churched man. He would not go to church with my mom, my sister, and me. He had been lied to by a preacher, and from that point on, he never trusted preachers again. The only times we saw him in church was if I was in town preaching or my brother-in-law was preaching. He trusted us. So this man, who had learned not to trust preachers, was a man of such honesty and integrity, that a used car salesman would let him just drive off the lot with whatever car he wanted. He taught me the same lesson that the apostle wants us to learn right here.

I may have learned to preach from preachers. I may have learned to think from professors. I may have learned theology from theologians. But I learned honesty from a carpenter/truck driver with an eighth-grade education, who simply let his yes be yes and his no be no.

Is anyone among you in trouble? Let them pray. Is anyone happy? Let them sing songs of praise. Is anyone among you sick? Let them call the elders of the church to pray over them and anoint them with oil in the name of the Lord. And the prayer offered in faith will make the sick person well; the Lord will raise them up. If they have sinned, they will be forgiven. Therefore confess your sins to each other and pray for each other so that you may be healed. The prayer of a righteous person is powerful and effective. Elijah was a human being, even as we are. He prayed earnestly that it would not rain, and it did not rain on the land for three and a half years. Again he prayed, and the heavens gave rain, and the earth produced its crops.

—James 5:13–18

This is an amazing section of Scripture. Too often we focus only on one part of it. So, let me break this down into three elements addressed here.

1. The Healing of the Body

The apostle starts with the healing of the body. "Is anyone among you sick?" He then goes on to establish a pattern for dealing with sickness, and this is a pattern that we often misunderstand. The apostle tells us to "pray" and "anoint."

Pray

This is really a pretty obvious call from the apostle. We should pray for the intervention of God in the lives of all those who are sick. God is still a miracle-working God! I believe this with all my heart. God can heal in ways that man cannot even begin to understand. Therefore, when someone is sick we should, and must, pray for God to heal. This prayer should be prayed in faith, believing that God can bring this type of healing. However, there is a word of caution to be spoken here: God can always heal, but God does not always choose to heal.

There is a horrible theology out there today that claims that God will *always* heal people who have enough faith. This insidious teaching has caused far too much harm to the church. Think logically for a moment. If it were true that God *always* heals people, then folks with good faith would never die.

I heard a preacher one time say that, since he had faith, he was going to "die healthy"! That is the most ridiculous, preposterous, heretical, shallow, misguided, stupid thing you could ever say. No one has ever died healthy. The writer of Hebrews makes this abundantly clear: "People are destined to die once, and after that to face judgment" (Heb. 9:27). All people will die at some point. It is a natural part of life, since sin entered this world. So remember that prayer is powerful and miracles do happen, but you cannot demand or presume on the healing hand of God.

Anoint

There are two words for *anoint* in the New Testament. The one we are most familiar with is the word *chrio*, which is the root word for Christ. This word is defined as: "to consecrate to an office or religious service."[1] This is the sacred word used to describe holy rites or moments that indicate the setting aside of something or someone for sacred purpose or holy office. This is not the word used by James in this verse.

Instead, James used the word *aleipho*. This means "to oil (with perfume)."[2] This word is not considered sacred and carries with it a connotation of treatment as in medicine. What the apostle was actually teaching was that we are to pray over the sick, believing that God can heal them, *while* we are treating the sick with the very best medical treatment we can find.

So, faith and reason work together! Using reason does not indicate a lack of faith nor does faith negate the need for human reason. God gave you a soul and a brain—so use both!

2. The Healing of the Soul

The apostle then went to an unexpected place: "If they have sinned, they will be forgiven." He carried the thought even further to say, "Therefore confess your sins to each other and pray for each other so that you may be healed." Healing is so much more than just being delivered from some physical ailment or handicap. Healing is deeper than that. God is sometimes willing to heal the body miraculously, but God is always looking to heal the soul miraculously. This healing of the soul is just not considered as exciting as healing of the body. Testimonies of folks who have had their bodies healed miraculously make great subject matter for books and movies. The healing of a soul is less visible, more internal, and less glamorous, but it is nonetheless miraculous. This is what God really wants to do in us. He desires to take our broken, sickened souls and raise them to a place of miraculous healing and health.

3. The Healing of the Community

Finally, note the illustration that the apostle used here. He spoke of Elijah praying and holding back the rains over all Israel. Why did he do that? Simple! Israel, specifically the king, had sinned. The soul of the nation was marred in sin and that caused great physical distress to the nation. When the soul is marred in sin, the refreshing rains of the Holy Spirit are blocked out, and eventually the landscape of our spiritual lives becomes a desert wasteland. This can happen to an entire community, an entire state, and an entire nation. It is by the faithfulness of a few that the rains of the Holy Spirit are restored to the many.

When the apostle tells us that "the prayer of a righteous person is powerful and effective," and then follows that truth with the story of Elijah praying that the rains would return to Israel, it is not a coincidence. I believe we are being called to be the Elijahs of our day. Praying constantly that God would bring redemption and refreshing upon the entire culture in which we live. We are called to be the ones who *anoint* this people and this land with the "perfume" of God's presence.

We accomplish all this simply by being God's people. "The prayer of a righteous person is powerful and effective."

So be a righteous person.

So be a praying person.

God will make you a powerful and effective person.

35

My brothers and sisters, if one of you should wander from the truth and someone should bring that person back, remember this: Whoever turns a sinner from the error of their way will save them from death and cover over a multitude of sins.

—James 5:19–20

This should be in the running for your life verse. You know, I have been preaching now for more than twenty-five years, and I have been in church steadily almost my entire life, and I cannot think of a single sermon preached on this verse. Sadly, even by me. (I will remedy that soon!) This is the core of who we are. This is the core of what we should be doing.

All too often, we simply hide ourselves away from the world around us, afraid that somehow if we touch them, we will catch the sin disease they have. Well, let me put your mind at ease. You can't catch what you already have. That disease of sin that you are trying so hard to avoid already runs through your veins. It is the devil that plants that fear inside of you in an attempt to render you useless in the expansion of the kingdom of God. So, while we shouldn't be frequenting places of poor reputation or attending parties with poor intentions, we also should not be avoiding people who are not like us. Instead we should be reaching out to them, especially those who once shared our faith and for whatever reason, have decided to walk away from their faith. Those people have history with us. While that history may make it more difficult to reach them, it shows that there is some level of belief within them. They believed once, so they can believe again. So keep trying. Even if you need to keep some space between you and them, don't give up completely!

Listen to the final words of this letter: "Whoever turns a sinner from the error of their way will save them from death and cover over a multitude of sins." How can that not be our goal? This is not just a spiritual, eternal promise; it is a present reality. When we turn a sinner from their sinful ways, we can literally save them from physical death caused by their spiritual rebellion. Sin is perfectly designed to kill. When we get people away from it, we save them from what is killing them. Furthermore, when we bring them into a right relationship with the person of God, the Word of God, the blood of Jesus, and the power of the Holy Spirit, their lives begin to change. As their lives change, the sins of their past slowly fade from the memory of all those around them. They are, over time, covered over by the newer, better version. The old ways are gone, and new ways have taken hold. The old patterns are gone, and new patterns have taken hold. As the apostle Paul puts it, "Therefore, if anyone is in Christ, the new creation has come: The old has gone, the new is here!" (2 Cor. 5:17).

Oh, that this would be the battle cry of the church!

No more political movements.

No more angry picketing.

No more fearful hiding beneath our pristine crosses.

No more insulting rhetoric designed to run off those not like us.

Just the simple goal of turning "a sinner from the error of their way."

That would be beautiful!

That would be awesome!

That would be the church acting like the Christ we say we serve!

And that would rock the world!

Notes

Introduction

1. Spiros Zodhiates, *Hebrew-Greek Key Word Study Bible: New American Standard Bible* (Chattanooga, TN: AMG Publishers, 1990), 1636.

2. H. D. M. Spence and Joseph S. Exell, *The Pulpit Commentary* (Grand Rapids, MI: Wm. B. Eerdmans Publishing Company, 1950), v.

3. Spence and Exell, *The Pulpit Commentary*, v.

Devotion 1

1. James Strong, *The New Strong's Exhaustive Concordance of the Bible* (Nashville, TN: Thomas Nelson Publishers, 1984), 77.

Devotion 5

1. J. Vernon McGee, *Thru the Bible* (Nashville, TN: Thomas Nelson Publishers, 1983), 638.

Devotion 7

1. H. D. M. Spence and Joseph S. Exell, *The Pulpit Commentary* (Grand Rapids, MI: Wm. B. Eerdmans Publishing Company, 1950), 5.

2. James Strong, *The New Strong's Exhaustive Concordance of the Bible* (Nashville, TN: Thomas Nelson Publishers, 1984), 36.

3. Spence and Exell, *The Pulpit Commentary*, 6.

4. J. Vernon McGee, *Thru the Bible* (Nashville, TN: Thomas Nelson Publishers, 1983), 644.

Devotion 19

1. James Strong, *The New Strong's Exhaustive Concordance of the Bible* (Nashville, TN: Thomas Nelson Publishers, 1984), 11.

Devotion 21

1. James Strong, *The New Strong's Exhaustive Concordance of the Bible* (Nashville, TN: Thomas Nelson Publishers, 1984), 47.
2. Strong, *The New Strong's Exhaustive Concordance of the Bible*, 31.
3. Strong, *The New Strong's Exhaustive Concordance of the Bible*, 33.

Devotion 22

1. J. Vernon McGee, *Thru the Bible* (Nashville, TN: Thomas Nelson Publishers, 1983), 659.

Devotion 25

1. James Strong, *The New Strong's Exhaustive Concordance of the Bible* (Nashville, TN: Thomas Nelson Publishers, 1984), 12.

Devotion 30

1. James Strong, *The New Strong's Exhaustive Concordance of the Bible* (Nashville, TN: Thomas Nelson Publishers, 1984), 56.

Devotion 34

1. James Strong, *The New Strong's Exhaustive Concordance of the Bible* (Nashville, TN: Thomas Nelson Publishers, 1984), 78.
2. Strong, *The New Strong's Exhaustive Concordance of the Bible*, 9.

Books in
Coffee with the Pastor Series

- Mike Hilson, *King David* (Indianapolis, IN: Wesleyan Publishing House, 2019).
- Mike Hilson, *The Book of James* (Indianapolis, IN: Wesleyan Publishing House, 2019).
- Mike Hilson, *Nehemiah* (Indianapolis, IN: Wesleyan Publishing House, coming in 2020).
- Mike Hilson, *The Book of Colossians* (Indianapolis, IN: Wesleyan Publishing House, coming in 2020).
- Mike Hilson, *The Books of 1–3 John* (Indianapolis, IN: Wesleyan Publishing House, coming in 2021).

Watch for these and other titles in the series at
www.wphstore.com.